BEEF

- CABBAGE
- CORN. MISO
- BALSAMIC
- SHALLOTS
- ASPARAGUS
- ROASTED
- WHIPPED POTATOES
- BUTTER — compound
- basil
- maitre d'hotel
- CHANTERELLES; shiitakes

LAMB

MINT
ROSEMARY
CINNAMON
POLENTA
GARLIC
RED WINE
FIDDLE HEADS
FAVAS
COUSCOUS
POMEGRANATE
ARTICHOKES

BASS

striped
RED WINE
lentils
mushrooms
caramelization
endive

GRILLED.
ROASTED.
BRAISED.

A NEW TURN IN THE SOUTH

A NEW TURN
IN THE SOUTH

SOUTHERN FLAVORS REINVENTED FOR YOUR KITCHEN

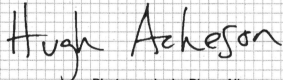

Hugh Acheson

Photographs by Rinne Allen

Clarkson Potter/Publishers

New York

Copyright © 2011 by Fried Pie, LLC
Photographs copyright © 2011 by Rinne Allen

All rights reserved.
Published in the United States by Clarkson Potter/Publishers, an imprint of
the Crown Publishing Group, a division of Random House, Inc., New York.

www.crownpublishing.com

www.clarksonpotter.com

CLARKSON POTTER is a trademark and POTTER with colophon is a
registered trademark of Random House, Inc.

Cataloging-in-Publication Data is available upon request
from the Library of Congress

ISBN 978-0-307-71955-3

Printed in China

Design by Laura Palese with Rinne Allen

Illustrations by Hugh Acheson, Rinne Allen,
Susan Hable, Carolyn Holmes, and Jordan Noel

10 9 8 7 6 5 4 3 2 1

First Edition

To Mary, Beatrice
Clementine.

You can find the
recipe for this
on page 69

CONTENTS

Weingut
Ökonomierat Rebholz
„Ganz Horn"
im Sonnenschein
2008
GG
Pfalz

HUGH ACHESON: FRIEND, CHEF, COMMUNITY TREASURE

Three decades ago, when I was considering moving to Athens to attend the University of Georgia Law School, I was talking through the pros and cons of the town with a young Atlanta lawyer who had just finished school there. For no apparent reason, he told me, "Bertis, one thing you do need to know about Athens—it's a gastronomic wasteland." He went on to say that as a college town, Athens had its fair share of acceptable burger, pizza, and burrito joints, but if one was looking for a good meal, it was not to be found in Athens.

How times change. Due in large part to Hugh Acheson and his distinctive and eclectic take on modern regional cooking, Athens has become a mecca for food lovers. Even ten years ago, when Hugh had the notion to open Five and Ten, there were no organic farms or sustainable agriculture concerns in our little town, and maybe one restaurant that could have survived in a city like Atlanta. And we still don't have a Whole Foods; we're only 150,000 people, and lots of those are college kids without much interest beyond the basics of the aforementioned college town cuisine. But Hugh, much to our delight, has led a culinary and cultural shift in Athens— centered at his flagship Five and Ten, and extended to The National, Gosford Wine, and Empire State South.

I remember my first meal at Five and Ten, on opening night in March 2000. Michael Stipe and I were both in town, happy to get the invitation to this spot we had been hearing about, and so we went expecting your basic finger food/cocktail party sort of function. But man were we wrong . . . full-on dinner, amazing tastes, and the dishes just kept coming. The restaurant was packed and we giddily looked around the room, repeatedly exclaiming, "Can you believe we're in Athens?" By 2002, Hugh was on the cover of *Food & Wine* as one of their Best New Chefs in America. Those of us in Athens were proud as hell of Hugh and his business; we already knew it was good from the start, but to see such acclaim from afar felt exceptional for the whole town. There he was in *Food & Wine*—chefs from New York, Seattle, Boston . . . and Athens, Georgia! The James Beard nominations started coming in a few years later and then Restaurant of the Year for Atlanta (Athens is not in Atlanta) by the *Atlanta Journal Constitution*. In 2007, Hugh's second restaurant, the National, opened and it was different in taste but similar in character: a warm, cozy, and stylish neighborhood restaurant where one can always find a great meal and a nice glass of wine. At both Five and Ten and the National, you always feel a real sense of community with those who are dining and those who are working. This sense of community is further heightened by the fact that many can walk home from both places, which is good.

Hugh's menus, like his restaurants and this cookbook, are a lot like Hugh: ever-changing yet consistent, with nuances and surprising flourishes, intense yet laid back, simple yet serious, never stuffy or pretentious or fussy. All of Hugh's creativity, from the bricks and mortar, textures, and lighting of the physical spaces themselves; to the words and images on his blog, on his menus, and in this book; to the main thing, the food itself, reflect his unique personality. If I had to point to one quality that sets Hugh apart and makes Hugh who he is, it is this: Hugh cares. He cares about his businesses, sure, the quality of the food and service and all of that. But he also cares about so much more—really cares. About politics, about his employees and their lives outside of work, about Athens and its many types of people, many of whom will never eat at any of his restaurants. He cares about the quality of our community's schools, not just because his own children attend them, but because all kids, regardless of where they come from, deserve a quality education and a chance for a decent future. Hugh not only cares deeply about these things, he acts and lives and demonstrates that caring through his commitment every day.

Hugh, although much younger than I am, has taught me and many others so much about the ever-growing sense of community in Athens. Not just the culinary community, the organic community, or any particular part of Athens. No, Hugh represents the concept that the whole community is important, and no one is a better example of giving back to our town than are Hugh and his restaurants. They steadfastly champion most everything good and caring and giving in Athens, from our public schools to sustainability and environmental concerns to critical social services agencies. Five and Ten for sure, but the National and Gosford too, and now Empire State South in Atlanta, but especially Hugh as a person; all of them embody and embrace the vital strands of this essential fabric of our town. And that is very good. We are no longer a culinary backwater, and we all have much to thank Hugh Acheson for: his food, his restaurants, and his presence.

Not long ago, I was somewhere in a small city in Italy, having a wonderful meal in a special and memorable restaurant, being served by waiters who had been with the chef-owner for several decades. And it hit me: Hugh is still so young. His best work is still ahead of him. Only ten years in, with who knows what is to come, Hugh Acheson is already doing great work that will only get better from here. Sitting there in Italy, I could picture myself, years from now, back home at Five and Ten, with lots of the same crew from the earliest days enjoying another tremendous meal. It was a pleasant and reassuring little epiphany. May it only come to pass. And whether you are one of the regulars like me, lucky enough to eat at Hugh's places, just down the street, all the time, or if you have yet to make it to Athens, you are in for a treat as you experience this volume celebrating Hugh's first decade. But be sure to leave time for a walk after dinner.

BERTIS DOWNS
MANAGER OF R.E.M.

I AM FROM OTTAWA, CANADA, and have spent almost a third of my life cooking food inspired by the Southern United States.

To me this is a happily strange situation. I have lived in the South three different times in my life; the third began in 2000 with the opening of Five and Ten in Athens, Georgia, and is still in full force. I have fallen hard for the place—for fried chicken; the railway trestles; the panoply of music, folk art, and front-porch living; and, most important, for the agrarian landscape. Agriculture has played a dominant role in Georgia for more than two and a half centuries, and it remains the most important sector of the economy today. None of my restaurants would exist without tomatoes from Woodland Gardens, eggs from Jan at Hope Springs Farm, or grits from Mills Farm.

When I was first living in Atlanta, my life as an eleven-year-old didn't really include a complete interpretation of place, but I do remember some specific Southern things entering into the fold: my step-grandmother's fried okra, my stepfather's collards, the teenage murmurs around the local pool about a great band from Athens (R.E.M.), the dogwood trees on my walk to school, the neighbors' calming drawl, Apalachicola oysters from the Gulf, and the Varsity, Atlanta's famous drive-in.

My education in food and Southern culture continued when at age thirteen I moved with my mother and stepfather from Atlanta to Clemson, a small college town in the South Carolina Piedmont: from barbecue at the Esso Club to my mother's chicken piccata and tomato aspic (straight from the pages of *Gourmet* and *Bon Appétit*), to hanging out at Subway, watching the punk-rock guys make Subway clubs while listening to Hüsker Dü. Sometimes they would give me the privilege of slicing the sandwich meats in the back room, a prelude to my later job in Ottawa's Cantor's Deli, where I left a small piece of the tip of my finger thanks to a state-of-the-art slicer. On home football game Saturdays, I roamed Death Valley's parking lots, painting orange tiger paws on fans' cheeks for donations. This was probably the first sign of my entrepreneurial spirit, and my introduction to college football and tailgating in the South. Clemson also had Mary, who would later become my wife and the inspiration behind such Five and Ten staples as Frogmore Stew and boiled peanuts.

After two years in Clemson, I returned to Ottawa and finished high school while living at my dad's, where canned wax beans and fish sticks were cherished for their simplicity and, no doubt, their convenience. My father did, and still does, have a great fondness, passed on to me, for good bread, Caesar salad, and oranges. I continued on my self-guided course of gastronomic enlightenment through high school, cooking at delis and restaurants. I then enrolled in Concordia University in Montreal, where I quickly realized that my backup plan of having a skilled trade was about to come in handy: I could cook, and that would pay the rent on a small apartment. I began to grow weary of political philosophy, my intended major, and cooking had my full attention. At nineteen, I dropped out of school and went to work in restaurants full-time.

Meanwhile, Mary and I reconnected, struck up a long-distance relationship, and moved together to Ottawa after she finished her undergraduate degree at Indiana University in 1994. There I landed a job at Café Henry Burger under Robert Bourassa and then at Maplelawn Café under Rob MacDonald, two classically trained chefs who profoundly influenced me, a guy with a monobrow, a chip on his shoulder, and an impatient wit. They taught me the fundamentals of French technique, which forms the foundational blocks of everything I cook today. Two years later, in

1996, Mary and I were married in Charleston, South Carolina, on our way from Canada to her native Athens, where she would pursue a graduate degree at the University of Georgia.

When we arrived in Athens, I got a job running a kitchen at a local restaurant and tried to soak up everything I could about Southern culture. It was a pretty bright time, with the Olympics in Atlanta and the economy purring. I was the young, trained chef in a small town, trying to find local ingredients, from goat cheese to grits to eggs and meats. The South, like the rest of the United States, was still in the grip of convenience, prepackaged, and fast food, which resulted in a homogenization of daily meals. All along, the sorghum maker, the grit grinder, the tomato farmer, and the country-ham guy were in our own backyards, and I was determined to make people aware of that again. The timing was just right: a new national fascination with regional foods was especially taking hold in the South.

I was in love with Athens but felt like I needed more training, so Mary and I moved in 1998 to San Francisco, where I worked at the restaurants Mecca and Gary Danko. When we returned to Athens two years later to open Five and Ten, I found myself in a unique position. I had a lot of classic technique in my repertoire and had ultra-credible experience in great restaurants. And while my Southern friends and family had their mothers' recipes to preserve and pass down, I had a relatively blank slate to interpret Southern food my way: to take a fresh approach and turn the traditions on their heads a little bit.

Not everything on the menu in my restaurants is Southern. Five and Ten incorporates a vast mix of cuisines but always with a Southern stamp: French sauces blanket Southern braises; Greek flavors season coastal mahimahi; grits pair with osso buco. At the National, a Mediterranean restaurant in downtown Athens I opened in 2007, the cuisines of Spain and northern Africa inform chef Peter Dale's menu, but it too has a Southern accent. At Gosford, my Athens wine store, we sell Reed's Rocket Nutcrackers from southeast Georgia and cheeses from Sweet Grass Dairy in south Georgia alongside hand-picked wines from across the globe. Empire State South, the newest restaurant, in Atlanta, is a meat-and-three with the same attention to purveying and localism that marks everything I do.

Southern food presents a special challenge for me: to interpret its nuances, always with respect for the traditions, the land, and the history that fostered it. So this is the food I cook in the South. It is the food born from my time here. The recipes are also a map of how I like to eat: Vegetables take a very prominent role, salads and soups abound, sides are prized, and fish and meats are on the simple side.

Simple can be difficult, so we have to pay attention. Let's season right and judiciously use a pinch of salt here and a drizzle of olive oil there. Know that salt is not a spice, rather it is a palate opener. It pulls out sugar and moisture in food to make the food taste better. It does the same to your palate but if you use too much you can't fix it and have to start again. Should this happen, swear in a foreign language and calmly start over. At the end of the day it's food and you need to enjoy it. If it's a labor of love that you learn about every day, then you have figured out my secret: Food is a beautifully endless topic. Now, let's make some collards.

LIBATIONS

Lemonade with vanilla, mint & rosemary

Watermelon Limeade

A-team waiter sweet tea

MAKER'S MARK & SPICY GINGER SODA

EGGNOG with bourbon

PEACH MIMOSAS

HEIRLOOM BLOODY MARYS

SOUTHERN PIMM'S CUP

I grew up with cocktails being a part of life. Hugh Stevens, my dear late grandfather, would drink an old-fashioned every evening after work, one with real fruit and real rye whiskey. My grandmother on the other side, Freda Acheson, would have a rum drink with her pepper jelly and cream cheese snacks at the end of the day. My mother has a scotch and soda on most evenings. To them, the cocktail is a generational demarking point of the day. It signals the time to relax and put up your heels on the ottoman.

In the progressive artisan culture that is so prominent in food and beverage today, cocktails are often matched to the season and mood. They cool us in the summer and warm us in the winter. Cocktails need not have alcohol in them to be great and fitting libations. They just need to quench.

Here is a small collection of my favorites, five with and three without alcohol.

Lemonade with Vanilla, Mint & Rosemary

8 cups (2 quarts) cold water
8 large lemons
1 cup granulated sugar
10 sprigs of fresh mint
½ vanilla bean, scraped seeds and pod
1 sprig of fresh rosemary

The vanilla in this recipe cuts the acidity of the lemon, and the real vanilla specks make it an especially pretty drink.

Pour the water in a large pot over high heat and bring to a boil. While the water is coming to a boil, halve the lemons and juice them thoroughly. Place the juice and the juiced lemon halves in a large heat-proof nonreactive pot. Add the sugar, 2 sprigs of mint, the vanilla seeds and pod, and the rosemary.

Pour the boiling water over the mixture. Stir carefully and let sit for 20 minutes. Stir well again and strain out the solids, then discard them and pour the lemonade into Mason jars or a large pitcher and keep refrigerated until people get thirsty.

To serve, pour the lemonade over ice in tall glasses, garnish each with a mint leaf, and sit on a porch.

MAKES 2 QUARTS; OR SERVES 8

PHOTO NOT
TO SCALE

Watermelons abound in Georgia. The only problem is fitting them in the fridge. This recipe can plow through half a watermelon pretty quickly, allowing the other half a little wiggle room in the fridge.

I do have a fancy blender at work, but at home I have an Osterizer workhorse that is about twenty years old and works great.

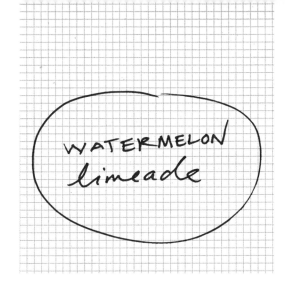

● ● ●● ● ●● ● ●● ●● ● ● ●● ● ●● ●● ● ●● ● ● ● ●● ● ●

Make a simple syrup by combining the sugar with 1 cup water in a small saucepan over low heat. Bring to a boil, reduce the heat, and simmer until the sugar is completely dissolved. Remove from the heat and let cool.

Place the watermelon in a blender, making sure to tightly ram the cubes down so the blender can do its magic. Puree the watermelon into watermelon water. Pour it into a pitcher and add the lime juice. Add 3 tablespoons of the simple syrup and reserve the rest for another use.

To serve, fill 6 pint glasses with ice and pour the watermelon limeade into each, up to an inch from the top. Top each glass with soda water and garnish with a slice of lime.

SERVES 6

½ cup fine turbinado sugar

4 cups cubed watermelon flesh

½ cup freshly squeezed lime juice (see Note)

1 cup soda water

6 slices of lime, for garnish

NOTE: there are citrus juicers that look like giant garlic presses. They are ingeniously simple. At the fancier stores they come in fancy packaging and pretty enamel colors and cost about fifteen to twenty dollars. the same thing in simple metal is $2.99 around the corner at our mexican grocery store.

A-team waiter sweet tea

1 tablespoon loose black tea
¾ cup granulated sugar
8 leaves of fresh mint
4 slices of lemon

Tea in the South doesn't arrive at the table hot. It isn't something to mix with milk and honey. Please don't flavor it with raspberry, or load it with açaí or other superfoods. Tea is sweet iced tea. Tea should not be so sweet as to strip tooth enamel. Tea is not made with green tea or anything fancy. It is simple caffeinated black tea with sugar and ice.

The A-Team are my loyal, dedicated, skilled, and selfless waitstaff who have been with me for years. They are our front line of smiles and smarts. When they finally leave Five and Ten, Paul, Steve, Bob, Toni, and Joe will carry with them the ability to make great iced tea.

This recipe can be doubled or tripled very easily. You will need two nice clean quart jars.

Pour 4 cups cold water into a kettle and bring to a boil. Add the black tea to one clean quart container and add the sugar to the other.

When the water is boiling, pour 2 cups of it over the tea and 2 cups of it over the sugar. Gently stir the sugar and water to combine and then cover both quart containers. Let the tea steep for 10 minutes (a rather long time in the tea world, but it will be diluted with an equal amount of sugar water).

Strain the steeped tea into the sugar water and let cool.

Fill 4 tall glasses with ice and pour the tea into each glass. Garnish with 2 mint leaves and a slice of lemon.

SERVES 4

This is a play on the classic spicy ginger ale and bourbon mix but with homemade ginger syrup. The simple way of making a syrup can be stretched into other cocktail and dessert applications as well. Maker's is a solid bourbon, but Evan Williams, Bulleit, or Old Rip Van Winkle are other options. If you want a bourbon just for sipping, try Elijah Craig on the low end and a fifteen-year-old Pappy Van Winkle on the high end.

Maker's Mark
& Spicy Ginger
SODA

● ●

In a small saucepan, bring 1 cup water, the ginger, and the sugar to a boil. Turn off the heat and allow to steep and cool for 1 hour. Strain off the ginger pieces and reserve the syrup.

Fill two 10-ounce highball glasses with ice to the top. In each glass, pour 3 ounces bourbon and 1 tablespoon ginger syrup, and stir. Add 2 slices of the peach and 2 ounces soda water to each glass. Stir gently and serve. The remaining ginger syrup will last for 2 weeks in the fridge.

SERVES 2

½ pound fresh ginger, peeled and finely grated
1 cup fine turbinado sugar
6 ounces Maker's Mark (or other bourbon of your choice)
4 slices of fresh ripe peach
4 ounces soda water

Eggnog with bourbon

Eggnog, the custard drink of the holidays, is easy to make. Traditionally made with rum and brandy, this distinctively Southern recipe is served with bourbon instead.

● ●

4 cups whole milk
1 cup granulated sugar
2 vanilla beans, split and scraped
Pinch of salt
8 eggs, separated
1½ cups Maker's Mark bourbon
½ cup light rum
1 cup heavy whipping cream
Freshly grated nutmeg

In a large saucepan, combine the milk, ¾ cup of the sugar, vanilla, and salt and cook over medium heat for 10 minutes, stirring occasionally.

In a large bowl, whisk the egg yolks. Remove the milk mixture from the heat and slowly pour a small amount into the egg yolks to temper. Pour the remaining milk mixture into the yolks, stirring continually. Once the milk mixture and egg yolks are combined, pour the custard base into the saucepan and cook until the mixture coats the back of a wooden spoon, 10 to 12 minutes.

Strain, cool, and add the bourbon and the rum.

In a medium mixing bowl, whip the egg whites until stiff peaks begin to form. Set aside.

In a separate bowl, whip the heavy cream and the remaining ¼ cup of sugar, then slowly fold the whipped heavy cream and the whites together; fold them into the eggnog.

Ladle the nog into mugs or glasses and grate some nutmeg on top, before serving.

MAKES 3 QUARTS; OR SERVES 10 TO 12

how I view the holidays:

Peach mimosas

2 fresh peaches
½ cup freshly squeezed orange juice
1 bottle of cold cava (750 milliliters)
8 fresh mint leaves, finely minced

Fifteen years ago, Freixenet had a lock on the cava market, but in the last decade, distributors such as Olé Imports, Eric Solomon, Wines of Spain, and Jorge Ordoñez have begun pouring good, inexpensive bubblies. True Champagne is fine, too, but that's kind of like having a single malt with Coke.

Prepare an ice bath by filling a medium bowl half with water and half with ice. In a large pot, bring 2 quarts water to a vigorous boil. Carve a small, shallow "X" in the non-stem end of the peaches and carefully lower them into the boiling water. Cook for 45 seconds and remove the peaches to the ice bath.

When cool enough to handle, pull away the loosened skin of the peaches. Remove each peach pit and place the flesh in a blender with the orange juice. Puree until smooth. Evenly distribute the peach puree among 8 champagne flutes. Fill the flutes with cava and garnish with the mint.

SERVES 8

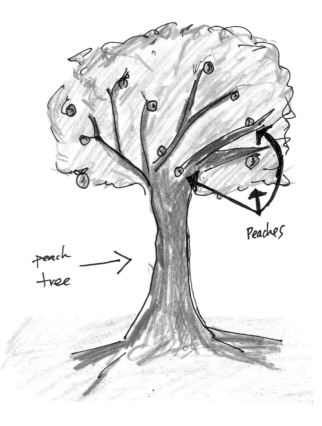

Peaches

peach tree →

This is a traditional Bloody Mary except that I peel and seed the tomatoes, season them with sea salt, and puree them with a dash of lemon juice. Garnishing with pickled okra, dill pickle, and a pickled jalapeño makes it even more special.

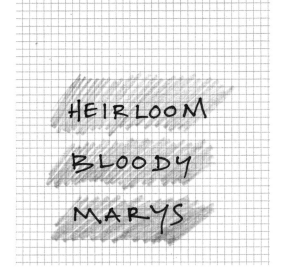

Place the tomato juice in a large pitcher. Add the Worcestershire, horseradish, pickle juice, vodka, and Tabasco to the pitcher and stir. Pour the Bloody Marys into 4 pint glasses filled with ice. Garnish with the pickle spears, jalapeños, okra, and black pepper to taste. Drink away.

SERVES 4

4 cups Tomato Juice (recipe follows)
½ teaspoon Worcestershire sauce
¼ teaspoon prepared horseradish
½ cup dill pickle juice (use the liquid from the pickle jar)
6 ounces vodka
2 teaspoons Tabasco sauce
4 dill pickle spears
4 pickled jalapeño chiles, whole
4 Pickled Okra (page 252)
Freshly ground black pepper

TOMATO JUICE

MAKES 4 CUPS

4 large Brandywine heirloom tomatoes (or any large heirloom variety)

1 tablespoon freshly squeezed lemon juice
½ teaspoon Maldon sea salt (see Box)

I like to use Maldon sea salt because it has a distinctive flakiness that differentiates it from more coarse sea salts. As an alternative to Maldon, you can use a fine sea salt.

Prepare an ice bath by filling a medium bowl half with water and half with ice. Bring 8 cups (2 quarts) water to a vigorous boil. Carve a small, shallow "X" on the bottom of each tomato without cutting too deeply into the flesh. Carefully lower the tomatoes into the boiling water. Cook for 1 minute and remove to the ice bath. When cool enough to handle, peel the skins off the tomatoes.

Cut the tomatoes in half along their equators. Gently squeeze out most of the seeds (it's okay if some remain). Place the tomato halves in a blender and puree for 30 seconds or until smooth. Add the lemon juice and salt. Taste and adjust lemon juice and salt if necessary.

heirloom bloody mary

Sometimes we just need to let loose. Don't confuse letting loose with losing all your smarts. It's actually just about relaxing, and that's why we in the South have front porches. When it's ten o'clock on Thursday night, still 94 degrees Fahrenheit outside, that's when I want a Pimm's Cup.

Pimm's No. 1, a British, gin-based aperitif liquor, has a light and airy, thirst-quenching character. Using Blenheim spicy ginger ale, which is made in Hamer, South Carolina, gives this version a Southern kick.

Southern Pimm's Cup

Fill two pint glasses with ice, then evenly divide the cucumbers, strawberries, and mint between the two glasses. Squeeze the lemon slices into the glasses and add the Pimm's, lemonade, and ginger ale. Stir well and serve.

SERVES 2

10 thin slices of cucumber

2 strawberries, hulled and cut in thin rounds

4 fresh mint leaves, torn into small pieces

4 slices of lemon

6 ounces Pimm's No. 1

4 ounces lemonade (see page 22) or if store-bought, go with Simply Lemonade

4 ounces spicy ginger ale (like Blenheim)

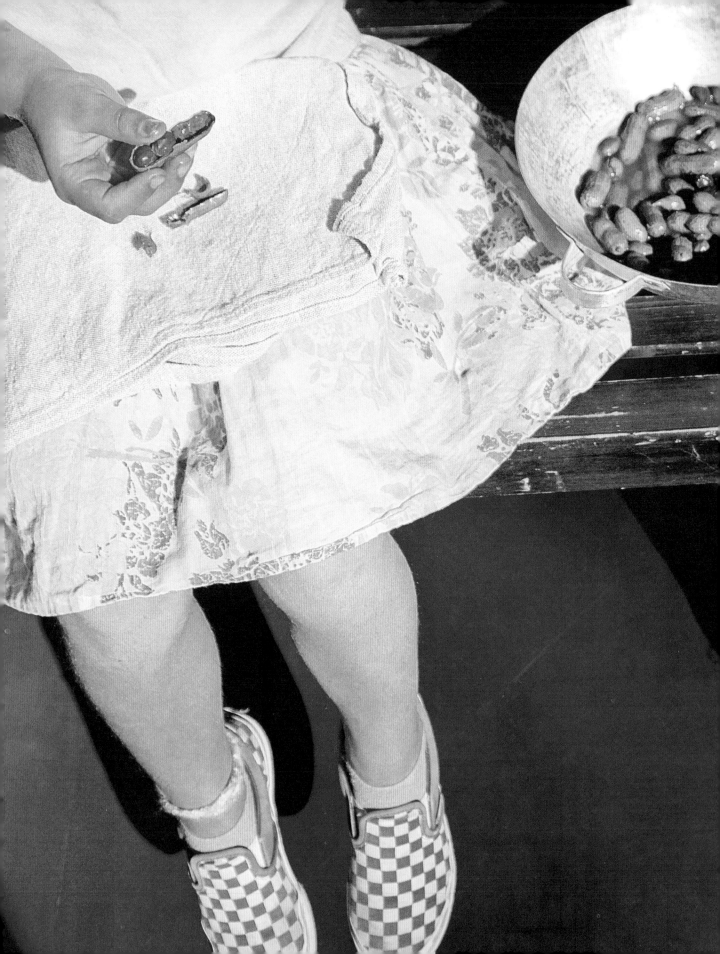

COUNTRY HAM with chilied mango

MARINATED ANCHOVIES with grapefruit & pepper

PIMIENTO CHEESE

MEDJOOL DATES stuffed with Parmagiano-Reggiano & Celery

PICKLED SHRIMP

BOILED-PEANUT HUMMUS

TOMATO ASPIC

BRESAOLA

DEVILED EGGS

I love it when a Five and Ten regular brings in a group of first-timers and orders marinated anchovies with grapefruit and pepper, telling his guests, "You have to try these. They sound weird but they're soooo good." Snackies are foods that satiate us so we don't fill up on bread. They match well with bubbles and martinis, gimlets and Chablis. Snackies, together with put-ups (see page 246), are the foods to lay out at the beginning of a lavish meal. Or they can make up what we call at home a "summer supper," when everything is pulled from the fridge to create a simple dinner—cut vegetables, pickles, pimiento cheese, hummus, cured meats, deviled eggs, and cheeses.

country ham with chilied mango

½ pound boneless country ham, thinly sliced

1 ripe mango, peeled, pitted, and diced

½ teaspoon freshly ground red pepper flakes

12 leaves of fresh arugula

1 tablespoon extra-virgin olive oil

When Allan Benton of Madisonville, Tennessee, talks about ham, we all swoon. Allan is a revered curer and smoker of country hams who, like a small handful of fellow American producers, has borrowed a trick or two from the wonders of Italian prosciutto production. Benton's, La Quercia, Colonel Bill Newsom's, Meacham's, and Broadbent's are all examples of country hams that we are eating "raw" and with great zeal. It used to be that all country hams were smoked and cooked, even after curing, as opposed to prosciutto and Serrano hams, which are served simply cured. Order an NSCH (new-school country ham!) whole for the holidays, or, like me, every Monday. They all have their differences, some being saltier, some smokier, and some more aged and nuanced.

Artisanal charcuterie continues to be a major part of Southern foodways. This particular combination is sweet and spicy and makes for a lovely start with Champagne or prosecco.

Arrange the country ham on a large platter. Place the mango in a small bowl and season with the red pepper flakes. Scatter the seasoned mango over the ham and arrange the arugula on top. Drizzle with olive oil and eat.

SERVES 6

How to cut a mango

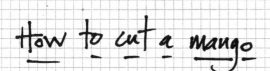

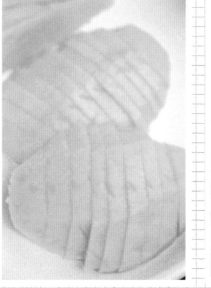

SouTHERN Community!

The South is a mosaic of many communities and when relationships are forged they last a long time.

Several years ago, I called Allan Benton, of Benton's Smoky Mountain Country Ham in Madisonville, Tennessee, to set up an account with him and get some ham. He knew my name and was happy I had called. The ham was delivered in its smoky, oil-stained box, the first of many such boxes that the restaurants would get over the next eight years. When the first shipment of aged hams was nearly exhausted I called again and Allan answered.

"Allan, this is Hugh Acheson at Five and Ten in Athens."

"Now Hugh, we know each other now and you just have to say, 'This is Hugh.'"

I was a little taken aback, but it taught me something quickly about Southern community. I had already been accepted into Allan's community, and formalities were no longer necessary. Such is life in the South.

This is a very simple way to embellish marinated white anchovies, the Spanish variety that are cooked, vinegary, and packed in oil. Marinated anchovies are not for Caesar salads, pizzas, or tomato sauce. These little beauties are a snack unto themselves. Pairing their puckery vinegar marinade with great olive oil, ruby red grapefruit, and freshly ground black pepper enhances their intrinsic flavor. Although I try to direct people away from the processed, manipulated, and ultrarefined packaged foods, there are some packaged items out there, such as marinated anchovies, that merit our attention. In this age of convenience, I want to relish in the right convenience items, and here they are paired with fruit, nature's best ready-to-eat offering! If you have trouble finding the anchovies at your local market you could order them from online sources such as Amazon.com or Tienda.com, or use Pickled Shrimp (page 51) as a substitute.

MARINATED ANCHOVIES WITH GRAPEFRUIT & PEPPER

1 large ruby red grapefruit
16 marinated white anchovy halves
½ teaspoon freshly ground black pepper
1 tablespoon extra-virgin olive oil

Using a sharp paring knife, cut off the top half inch and the bottom half inch of the grapefruit. Rest the bottom of the fruit on the cutting board and cut off the pith and skin, moving from top to bottom. Once you have the fruit ready to go, cup it in your hand and carefully run the knife blade between each segment, stopping at the center of the fruit, to free the segments from their skins. Do not use too much pressure when cutting; instead, let the sharpness of the knife work for you. Place the segments in a small bowl, and when all of the segments have been removed, squeeze the juice on top.

Arrange the anchovies and the grapefruit segments on a plate in an alternating pattern. Sprinkle with the freshly ground pepper and then drizzle with the olive oil. Serve immediately.

SERVES 4

Pimiento Cheese

Pimiento cheese was a hurdle I couldn't get over until about ten years ago. I just didn't like mayo and cheese together; they were too similar in texture. But after my wife, Mary, insisted on it, I started experimenting and came up with a winner. Now I can't get through the week without at least one great sourdough and pimiento cheese sandwich with Pickled Okra (page 252) on the side. It's a versatile component as well. Serve it as a sandwich, a spread for crisp toasted breads, a filling for celery, a topping for burgers, or in finished grits.

1 pound sharp white cheddar, such as an 18-month-old

2 large red bell peppers, roasted, peeled, seeded, and diced

½ cup Mayonnaise (recipe follows, or Duke's in a pinch)

1 teaspoon Dijon mustard

½ tablespoon smoked sweet Spanish paprika

Pinch of cayenne

½ teaspoon kosher salt

Grate the cheddar by hand to a medium shred and place in a large bowl. Add the peppers, mayonnaise, mustard, paprika, cayenne, and salt and mix thoroughly with a wooden spoon.

MAKES 4 CUPS

MAYONNAISE

1 whole egg
2 egg yolks
2 tablespoons freshly squeezed lemon juice

1 teaspoon Dijon mustard
1 cup vegetable oil
1 cup olive oil

In a stainless-steel mixing bowl set over a bowl of salted ice, whisk together the egg, egg yolks, lemon juice, and mustard. Slowly whisk in the vegetable oil and olive oil to emulsify. Immediately refrigerate and use within 2 days.

MEDJOOL DATES STUFFED WITH PARMIGIANO-REGGIANO & CELERY

8 medjool dates

1 celery stalk

2 tablespoons extra-virgin olive oil

1 teaspoon freshly squeezed lemon juice

1 tablespoon chopped fresh flat-leaf parsley

Pinch of sea salt

2-ounce piece of Parmigiano-Reggiano, finely grated

1 teaspoon good balsamic vinegar

This snackie counters the richness of the dates with the sharpness of Parmigiano-Reggiano and the crunch of celery. It's a great match, as the sweetness finds a nice savory foil to dance with. A little date goes a long way though, so think accordingly.

This is not the time to go cheap on the Parmigiano. True Parmigiano-Reggiano is a testament to the old guard. Rules regarding its production have not changed nor economized through technology. The results are a hard cow's-milk cheese, unpasteurized, aged for at least eighteen and up to forty-eight months. Most grocery stores have decent Parmigiano nowadays, but for the really great ones, find a cheesemonger or a great Italian food shop, or go online to Murray's Cheese or Cowgirl Creamery. It costs money, but great Parmigiano is worth every penny and keeps for a number of months in your fridge.

* *

Carefully slit each date lengthwise. Pull out the pits and discard. Using your fingers like you are opening a book, open the date a little to create a space for the filling.

Peel the celery with a sharp peeler. Discard the stringy peelings and then cut the celery into thin bias cuts about ¼ inch thick and 1 inch long. Place the celery in a small bowl and add 1 tablespoon of the olive oil, the lemon juice, parsley, and salt. Toss well and add the Parmigiano.

Grab about 1½ tablespoons of the stuffing between your thumb and forefinger and place a date in your other hand, with the open area facing out. Place the stuffing in the date and gently close your hand around the fruit to secure the filling. Place the stuffed dates on a platter and drizzle with a touch of balsamic vinegar and the remaining olive oil. Serve.

SERVES 4

I love the invigorating jump of vinegar on the palate that pickles give. These shrimp are a great hors d'oeuvre for a warm summer evening matched with a nice chenin blanc from the Loire in France or from South Africa. Chenin has a great little uptick of sweetness at the end of your sip that contrasts well with the spice and richness of the shrimp.

At Five and Ten, we use shrimp from Port Royal, South Carolina, or Tybee Island, Georgia. Shrimp are one of the few sea yummies that freeze well, so don't hesitate to buy a five-pound block of frozen shrimp if you can't find it fresh off the boat.

PICKLED SHRIMP

2 tablespoons Old Bay seasoning

1 pound shrimp, peeled
(I like 26 to 30 count for this)

½ teaspoon celery seeds

¼ teaspoon allspice berries

½ teaspoon dried red pepper flakes

1 tablespoon sea salt

1 cup extra-virgin olive oil

⅓ cup freshly squeezed lemon juice

2 garlic cloves, minced

6 fresh bay leaves or 12 dry

¼ cup fresh flat-leaf parsley leaves, minced

½ medium Spanish onion, thinly sliced

* *

Prepare an ice bath by filling a medium bowl half with water and half with ice.

Bring a large pot of water to a boil. Add the Old Bay, then the shrimp and immediately reduce the heat to low. Cook for about 2 minutes, or until the shrimp are pink through and just cooked. Plunge the shrimp into the ice bath to cool, then drain and reserve them in the fridge.

Grind the celery seeds and allspice in a spice grinder and combine in a bowl with the red pepper flakes, salt, olive oil, lemon juice, garlic, bay leaves, and parsley. Stir.

In a clean, nonreactive container, layer the shrimp and the pickling liquid. Repeat. Cover and let sit in the fridge for 24 hours. In a pinch, you can do this all in a large sealable bag.

Serve with toothpicks and a pile of napkins, or incorporate into a pickled shrimp salsa.

MAKES 6 CUPS

We see "nonreactive" a lot in cookbooks and pretty much that just means not aluminum. Mixing acids (lemon juice) and aluminum can produce undesirable metallic flavors and discoloration.

A NOTE ABOUT SHRIMP:
Wild American Shrimp, from the East coast or the Gulf, are a precious commodity that we need to protect.

Buy domestic when you can. I adore the red shrimp from Brunswick, Georgia. They are super-tender and remind me of ebi, Japanese sushi shrimp. Early-season little brown shrimp are a delight as well. The term "green headless shrimp" just means uncooked little creatures lacking their noggins and not washed in a chemical preservative. Green is unadulterated. I love the white shrimp from Tybee Island, Georgia, which are brought in coolers to me by a man named Dan from March through August. He ambles in with his coolers and sells me fifty pounds at a time.

In 2008, when gas prices went through the roof, shrimpers could barely afford to take out their boats. This really hurt small brokers like Dan. Things have improved a little bit, but it still is a hard market. When you compete with farmed shrimp from Thailand, price becomes a monster issue with most buyers. What needs to change is the price-first mentality. Quality should reign supreme, and if it does, American shrimp win, hands down.

If you can't find fresh shrimp, don't be deterred. Shrimp are one of the few proteins that freeze well, so buy them from the freezer aisle if they are not in season. I usually bank on a quarter pound per person for a snack or appetizer and a third of a pound per person for a main course.

Ottawa, my hometown, has a very large Lebanese community, which means great inexpensive food on just about every corner. Hummus, a Lebanese staple, is traditionally made with whipped chickpeas, also known as garbanzo beans, which are blended with tahini and spices. Tahini is ground sesame and is available in better grocery and health food stores.

The South is not a hotbed of garbanzos, so I use what we have in abundance and love dearly: boiled peanuts. Creating their own lore, my daughters, Beatrice and Clementine, claim that finding four peanuts in one shell means good luck. They also call the shells "cradles" and the peanuts "peas."

Green peanuts are picked earlier than most peanuts, before the curing, or drying process (on the vine), begins. The season for green peanuts is late summer into mid-fall.

Out of green peanut season, you can use canned boiled peanuts. However, they lack the al dente resistance that you'll get from boiling your own. Matt and Ted Lee's BoiledPeanuts.com is a great source for canned peanuts and boiled peanut bumper stickers.

Serve boiled peanut hummus the same way you would traditional hummus: in a bowl surrounded with flatbreads, chips, celery, carrots, cucumber, sweet peppers, or whatever will scoop up the hummus. Salt the hummus carefully, as the boiled peanuts will be salty already.

Warning: this is the most addictive stuff in the book.

Boiled-Peanut Hummus

1 cup shelled Boiled Peanuts (recipe follows)
2 tablespoons tahini
1 medium garlic clove, minced
1 tablespoon freshly squeezed lemon juice
¼ teaspoon ground cumin
Tiny pinch of cayenne
2 tablespoons olive oil
Salt

Combine the boiled peanuts, tahini, garlic, lemon juice, cumin, and cayenne in a food processor and turn on low. Add the olive oil to emulsify. Add 2 tablespoons water to thin, and blend until the mixture is the consistency of spreadable hummus. Season with salt to taste.

MAKES 2 CUPS

recipe continues ⟶

BOILED PEANUTS

MAKES 2 QUARTS

¼ cup kosher salt
¼ cup cider vinegar
1 tablespoon Old Bay
  seasoning

2 star anise
1 pound raw, green peanuts
  in the shell

Put the salt, vinegar, and 1 gallon water in a big pot. Add the Old Bay and star anise, then the peanuts. Find a plate that is just smaller than the diameter of your pot. Place the plate on top of the peanuts to weigh them down and keep them under water. Bring the peanuts to a boil.

Reduce the heat to a simmer and cook for about 6 hours, or until the peanuts are very tender (open the shell and taste the peanut to test). Turn off the heat and transfer the peanuts to a large clean bowl. Serve immediately or store them in jars or sealable bags with some of the cooking liquid to keep them moist. They will keep in the fridge for about a week.

With an abundance of heirloom tomato varietals available at grocery stores and a panoply of seed choices at garden centers, we are seeing a nice sprint away from those red orbs that call themselves tomatoes. You know the ones: consistency of sponge, taste of antimatter.

Woodland Gardens, just next to the Athens airport, is our main tomato source. Celia, the treasured managing gardener there, brings us case after case of Black Krims, Brandywines, Cherokee Purples, and Mr. Stripeys.

An aspic is a gelatinized broth served as an appetizer or cubed into nice little garnishes for a whole poached salmon centerpiece, usually on a cruise ship's very large buffet. I think aspic got a bad name in the Jell-O era, when gelatin was only served sweetened and, if you were in the South, congealed around marshmallows. I love this recipe, but I remember our customers' reticence to order it when we first served it at Five and Ten. When they eat it, though, they see why we get excited about tomato Jell-O.

* *

Warm 1 tablespoon of the olive oil in a small nonreactive pot over medium heat. Add the shallot and sweat it for 5 minutes. Add the celery and cook for 5 more minutes over low heat. Add the tomato juice, parsley, lemon zest and juice, red pepper flakes, and ½ teaspoon sea salt. Cook for 10 minutes. Carefully puree the mixture in a blender and pass it through a fine strainer into a medium bowl.

Add the gelatin to the warm tomato broth, then pour the mixture back into the nonreactive pot and cook over medium heat. Bring to a simmer and turn off the heat. Add the basil to the mixture.

Pour the tomato sol (the warm gelatinized solution) into an 8 by 5-inch baking dish. Place it in the fridge and let it set for 4 hours or until it's gelled.

Place the cherry tomatoes in a small bowl and season with salt. Add the arugula, then dress with balsamic vinegar and the remaining tablespoon of olive oil. Scatter the croutons and ham over the aspic and garnish with the dressed tomatoes and arugula. Serve family style.

SERVES 4

Tomato aspic

2 tablespoons extra-virgin olive oil

1 shallot, minced

¼ cup minced celery

2 cups Tomato Juice (page 33)

1 teaspoon chopped fresh flat-leaf parsley

¼ teaspoon grated lemon zest

1 teaspoon freshly squeezed lemon juice

Tiny pinch of red pepper flakes

Sea salt

1 tablespoon powdered gelatin

1 tablespoon finely chopped fresh basil (cut into tiny squares, the prettier the better)

8 cherry tomatoes, such as Super 100s

¼ cup chopped arugula

1 teaspoon balsamic vinegar

½ cup Tiny Croutons (see page 163)

¼ cup finely minced country ham

Bresaola

1 pound center-cut beef tenderloin,
   one single center cut piece, trimmed
   of all connective tissue
2 cups kosher salt
½ cup unpacked light brown sugar
2 tablespoons fresh thyme leaves
2 tablespoons fresh marjoram leaves
2 tablespoons flat-leaf parsley leaves
½ tablespoon fresh tarragon leaves

Bresaola is Italian salt-cured beef. This version relies on high-quality beef, briefly cured and hand cut. I love serving it with some small cuts of crisp carrots, cold minted spring peas, and a simple horseradish crème fraîche. This is kind of a fancy snackie steak plate.

My neighbor Jim Okey, an accomplished cook who travels to Italy every year to make wine in Piedmont, brought me back a recipe for bresaola, which is now pretty famous in our kitchens. This is archetypal Italian cookery: reverential to great ingredients, thoughtful in minimal seasoning, and purposeful in end result.

To pull this off, you need to get some awesome beef. The good news is that through the wonders of artisanal farming and the Internet you can do that a lot more easily than you could ten years ago. You can get beautiful Piedmontese beef from Heritage Foods at HeritageFoods USA.com that would work really well in this recipe.

Pat the beef dry and set it aside in an 8 by 10 by 2-inch baking dish. Mix the salt and brown sugar together in a small bowl and set aside. Chop the thyme, marjoram, parsley, and tarragon, mix together, and spread evenly on a cutting board. Roll the beef into the herbs so they cling to the beef. Any remaining herbs can be folded into the salt-sugar blend.

Place the beef back in the baking dish and cover with the salt-sugar mixture. Cover the dish with plastic wrap and set in the fridge for 48 hours.

Remove the beef from the salt cure and scrape it clean. Rinse the beef briefly under cold water, then pat it dry. Slice very thin and serve.

SERVES 6

Sometimes we can wrap sound technique around a simple bite and make it so much better than most iterations, and that is the case with deviled eggs. I like the eggs boiled but not punished. I like the yolks smooth and silky and not chunky. I like the clean bite of the heat from the cayenne and a little hint of vinegar to mimic the hot sauce that usually is prescribed.

Deviled eggs need to have a kick or you have made stuffed eggs and left the devil out. Life gets boring without a little devilish influence.

8 eggs (2 extra in case of peeling trauma)
½ teaspoon kosher salt
1 teaspoon white vinegar
½ teaspoon smoked hot paprika
Pinch of cayenne
1 tablespoon Dijon mustard
2 tablespoons mayonnaise
½ teaspoon cider vinegar
1 tablespoon freshly squeezed lemon juice
Optional garnishes: chopped fresh chives, cooked lobster, cooked bacon, chopped ham, cooked chanterelles, Pickled Shrimp (page 51), and Pickled Okra (page 252)

About 12 hours before you cook the eggs, pull them out of the fridge, pick them up, and lay them on their sides, still in the carton. This will center their yolks for cooking and bring them to room temperature, the place where most civilized countries believe eggs should be stored.

Place the eggs in a heavy pot, cover by an inch with lukewarm water, and heat on medium high. Bring to a boil and then add ¼ teaspoon of the kosher salt and the teaspoon of white vinegar. Cover the pot and turn off the heat. Set a timer for 10 minutes. Meanwhile, prepare an ice bath by filling a medium bowl half with water and half with ice to cool the eggs once the timer goes off. At that point, remove the eggs to the ice bath and let them cool completely.

Gently crack the eggs by rolling them against a counter, using some pressure but just enough to crack the shells. Do this to all the eggs and then place them back in the water to soak for 30 minutes. This will allow the shells to be more easily removed. Peel the eggs carefully, then cut them in half with a sharp non-serrated knife, wiping down the knife each time to ensure clean cuts. Gently pry out the yolks into a medium bowl and set aside the whites.

Place the yolks in a food processor and add the remaining ¼ teaspoon of salt, the paprika, cayenne, Dijon mustard, mayonnaise, cider vinegar, lemon juice, and 1 tablespoon water. Process until smooth. Scrape the yolk filling into a sealable plastic bag, cut off a corner of the bag to make a ½-inch hole, and then pipe the yolk filling into the egg whites.

Garnish with chives or more paprika, cooked lobster, bacon, or ham, chopped shrimp or okra caviar, or pretty much anything you'd like.

SERVES 6

MEAL LEADERS:
first courses

1st

OYSTERS ON THE HALF SHELL with FOUR SAUCES

GOODTOWN OYSTERS (Bienville)

Crisp Sweetbreads with Baked Grits, Succotash & Tarragon Jus

CHANTERELLES on TOAST

Duck Confit with braised cabbage and star anise jus

Braised & Crisped PORK BELLY with CITRUS SALAD

Risotto with OKRA, COUNTRY HAM, BOILED PEANUTS, AND RAMPS

SOUTHERN CARBONARA   HUGH'S LOBSTER PIE

Fried green tomatoes with pickled shrimp & ranch dressing

Shrimp with celery, caviar, and buttermilk dressing

Yellow Grits with sautéed shiitakes, fried eggs, and salsa rossa

In Italy they begin their meals with small bites of antipasti and then pasta. In the Middle East...

they begin with mezze and then salads. In England they eat their salads later in the meal, confusing everyone. The Japanese begin with soup and finish with pickles. The French start with charcuterie and finish with cheese, making us all wonder how they live so long. In the Americas we seem to be still learning about how we want to eat and so we tend to be pretty flexible in meal style.

At my restaurants, I want the guests to dictate what type of experience they want to have. To some we are a very special occasion spot, to others we are in their daily meal plan. Some people have one course, others want us to craft them a five-course wine-paired meal. Let's be clear, though: I do have a perfect meal envisioned for you, as does any waiter worth his or her salt. We can often sense which guests want grilled chicken on their large salad before they even sit down, or which couple would love wine matches for a six-course celebration before the wine list has been glanced at.

When time permits, the perfect American home-entertaining meal is a small first course, followed by a small soup or salad, then a fish or meat course, and finally dessert. If we are feeling decadent we will have some cheese before the sweets. That's the way I want to eat but, given the multiple factors that all of us have to deal with these days, we rarely get that time to enjoy that ideal meal. The kids' bedtime, the traffic home from work, the line at the grocery store, various appointments . . . all of these impact that time at the table, which is why these first courses can also double as a complete dinner.

OYSTERS on the HALF SHELL with FOUR SAUCES

Some hungry seafarer pulls a barnacle shell from the ocean, cracks open the shell, and consumes the thing inside, only to find that it's delicious. He immediately yearns for eleven more "shells with treat inside" and eventually discovers how well they match tomato-horseradish sauce, a simple cracker, and a nice bottle of Champagne.

Luckily, we have five or six varieties of oysters on hand at Five and Ten all the time, including Malpeques from Prince Edward Island, Fanny Bays from British Columbia, and Apalachicolas from the Florida panhandle. We serve them simply, shucked and left in their bottom shells, briny and fresh with lemons, hot sauce, and a couple of classic oyster sauces. Cocktail sauce is always on hand at the restaurants and at home and I always love the slap of a bracing mignonette. Mignonettes are vinegar-based sauces typically containing black pepper and shallot. They are used sparingly because a little goes a long way.

recipe continues →

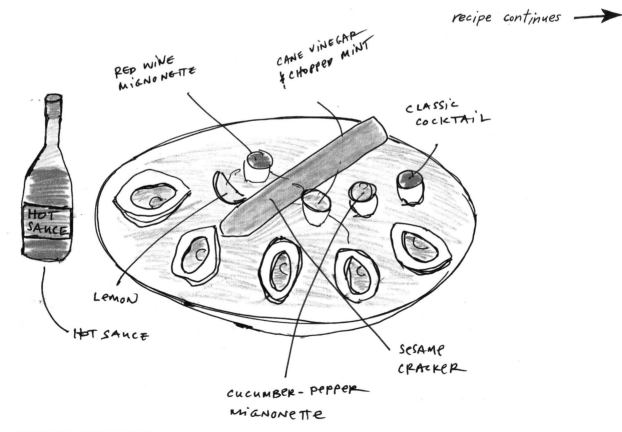

RED WINE MIGNONETTE

CANE VINEGAR & CHOPPED MINT

CLASSIC COCKTAIL

HOT SAUCE

LEMON

HOT SAUCE

SESAME CRACKER

CUCUMBER-PEPPER MIGNONETTE

this is my daughter BEATRICE shucking some oysters

FOUR OYSTER SAUCES

CLASSIC COCKTAIL SAUCE

MAKES 2 CUPS

3 plum tomatoes, cut in half, seeded and diced
½ cup ketchup
1 shallot, minced
2 teaspoons prepared horseradish
½ teaspoon grated lemon zest
1 tablespoon freshly squeezed lemon juice
1 teaspoon chile powder
1 teaspoon hot sauce

1 teaspoon Worcestershire sauce
1 tablespoon minced fresh flat-leaf parsley
½ teaspoon chopped fresh thyme leaves
½ teaspoon lightly packed light brown sugar
½ teaspoon kosher salt
¼ teaspoon freshly ground black pepper

Place the tomatoes, ketchup, shallot, horseradish, lemon zest, and lemon juice in a blender and puree for 10 seconds, or until smooth. Add the chile powder, hot sauce, Worcestershire, parsley, thyme, brown sugar, salt, and pepper and puree for another 10 seconds. This sauce will keep for 10 days in the fridge.

CUCUMBER-PEPPER MIGNONETTE SAUCE

MAKES ¾ CUP

¼ cup champagne vinegar
¼ cup dry sparkling wine
4 tablespoons minced cucumber

1 teaspoon freshly ground black pepper

In a small Mason jar, combine the vinegar, wine, cucumber, and pepper. Secure the lid and shake to blend. This sauce will keep in the fridge for 3 or 4 days.

RED WINE MIGNONETTE SAUCE

MAKES ¾ CUP

¼ cup good dry red wine
¼ cup red wine vinegar
2 tablespoons minced sweet onion

⅛ teaspoon dried mustard
⅛ teaspoon ground cumin
1 teaspoon minced fresh chives

In a small Mason jar, combine the wine, vinegar, onion, mustard, cumin, and chives. Secure the lid and shake to blend. This will keep for 1 week in the fridge.

CANE VINEGAR AND CHOPPED MINT SAUCE

MAKES ¾ CUP

½ cup cane vinegar (Philippine or American . . . I like Steen's Louisiana Cane Vinegar)

¼ cup apple cider
1 tablespoon minced shallot
2 teaspoons minced fresh mint

In a small Mason jar, combine the vinegar, cider, shallot, and mint. Secure the lid and shake to blend. This will keep for 2 to 3 days in the fridge.

GOODTOWN OYSTERS (Bienville)

There is an old line about oysters being good only in the months that end in R, but overnight shipping has made that obsolete. In July I can get great oysters from British Columbia, and in the winter I get them from Virginia. This recipe is versatile: If lobster is inexpensive, and what you prefer, use it in place of the shrimp. If you have a bunch of button mushrooms then by all means use those. Don't be afraid to try something new. I would want to drink this with a great simple lager like a Pabst Blue Ribbon, but let's go fancy and buy the bottles as opposed to the cans.

¼ pound bacon cut into small dice

½ medium sweet onion, peeled and minced

Pinch of salt

Pinch of cayenne

¼ teaspoon red pepper flakes

¼ cup (½ stick) plus 1 tablespoon unsalted butter

1 tablespoon freshly minced garlic

2 tablespoons all-purpose flour

1 cup whole milk

1 cup shiitake mushrooms, stemmed and diced

¼ pound American shrimp, peeled, deveined, and chopped into ½-inch pieces

1 teaspoon freshly squeezed lemon juice

¼ cup minced scallions, white and green parts

2 tablespoons chopped fresh flat-leaf parsley

2 egg yolks, lightly beaten

24 oysters, shucked but left in their deep cup

2 tablespoons fresh bread crumbs

8 cups rock salt (aka ice cream salt) for a good malleable surface to rest the oysters on

8 lemon wedges

Preheat the oven to 450°F.

First make the Bienville base. In a large fry pan over medium heat, cook the bacon until it's just about crisp and add the onion, salt, cayenne, and red pepper flakes. Cook for 5 minutes. Add 2 tablespoons of the butter and the garlic and cook for 2 minutes, then add the flour and cook for 2 more minutes while continually stirring.

Add the milk and stir well with a whisk. Reduce the heat to medium and add the mushrooms and the shrimp. Cook for 5 minutes, or until the mixture begins to thicken and set. Add the lemon juice, scallions, and parsley, then remove from the heat. While the mixture is still hot, whisk in the egg yolks and stir well. Pour onto a baking sheet to cool to room temperature.

Scoop about a teaspoon of Bienville base on top of each oyster and then add ⅛ tablespoon of butter and a pinch of bread crumbs on top. Pour half the rock salt into a baking sheet and nestle the oysters gently in the salt. This will keep the oysters from tipping over. Roast for 15 minutes.

Line a platter with the remaining rock salt, nestle the roasted oysters in the salt, and serve with the lemon wedges.

SERVES 8 (3 OYSTERS PER PERSON)

Sweetbreads are neither sweet nor breads. They are offal (or viscera from a butchered animal). The thymus sweetbreads are from the throat of a young cow and the pancreas sweetbreads are from around the heart. Both are great, but the heart sweetbreads tend to be rounder and larger.

Athens, Georgia, is not the easiest place in the world to sell offal. When I first put sweetbreads on the menu ten years ago, I had the waiters explain that they were "the best McNuggets you'll ever taste!"

This is a long process, and it takes patience, but the reward is totally worth it.

● ●

Preheat the oven to 325°F.

In a medium saucepan, over high heat, combine the water, milk, ¼ teaspoon salt, and grits. Bring to a boil. Stir well with a whisk to ensure that none of the grits are sticking. Reduce the heat to low, and switch to a wooden spoon, stirring every 5 minutes for 45 minutes, then remove the grits from the heat but leave them in the pot.

After the grits have cooled for 5 minutes, add 1 tablespoon of the butter, the egg yolks, and the cream and gently stir to combine. Butter an 8 by 8-inch ceramic baking dish and pour in the grits custard base. Insert this baking dish into a deep-sided roasting pan and place in the oven. Pour warm water into the roasting pan to create a water bath to insulate the grits. Bake for 30 minutes. Remove from the oven and set aside.

Raise the oven temperature to 425°F.

Place the sweetbreads in a medium pot and cover with cold water. Add 1 bay leaf, thyme, and celery. Place over medium heat, bring to a slow boil, then turn off the heat. Let the sweetbreads sit in the warm water for 10 minutes.

Remove the sweetbreads from the water and carefully remove the fat and connective tissue from around and between them. Cut the cleaned sweetbreads into 1-inch-thick slices and place in a bowl.

CRISP VEAL SWEETBREADS with baked grits, succotash & tarragon jus

1 cup cold water

1 cup whole milk

½ teaspoon kosher salt

½ cup stone-ground white hominy grits

2 tablespoons unsalted butter

3 egg yolks

1 tablespoon heavy cream

1½ pounds veal sweetbreads

2 bay leaves

1 branch of fresh thyme

½ cup finely minced celery

¼ teaspoon freshly ground black pepper

1 cup buttermilk

1 cup fine yellow cornmeal

1 tablespoon olive oil

1 shallot, minced

¼ cup dry vermouth

1 star anise

1 cup Chicken Stock (page 179)

1 teaspoon fresh tarragon leaves, chopped

1 cup Succotash (page 226)

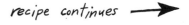 *recipe continues* ⟶

Season the sweetbreads with the remaining salt and the freshly ground pepper and then cover with the buttermilk.

Place the cornmeal in a large shallow baking dish.

Warm a large fry pan over medium-high heat.

Pull the sweetbreads out of the buttermilk and dredge through the cornmeal. Shake excess cornmeal from the sweetbreads and place the sweetbreads on a plate.

Add the remaining tablespoon of butter and the olive oil to the warmed fry pan. Add the sweetbreads and crisp off until golden, about 2 minutes per side. Remove the sweetbreads from the pan and place in a small baking dish. Place the baking dish in the oven for 3 minutes to finish cooking. Remove the baking dish from the oven and keep the oven on.

Discard the butter and oil in the fry pan and add the shallot to the pan. Cook over medium heat and deglaze with the vermouth. Add the star anise, 1 bay leaf, and chicken stock and reduce for 3 minutes. Whisk in the tarragon. Strain, discarding star anise, bay leaf, and shallot. Set aside.

Arrange 6 plates on a counter. Reheat the baked grits by placing them in the 425°F oven for 3 minutes. Warm the succotash in a pot over low heat, stirring frequently, and spoon 2 tablespoons onto each plate. Place about the same amount of baked grits on the plate next to the succotash and evenly arrange the sweetbreads among the plates. Drizzle with the tarragon jus and serve immediately.

SERVES 6

CHANTERELLES on TOAST

2 tablespoons extra-virgin olive oil

1 pound fresh chanterelles

2 tablespoons sherry vinegar

1 tablespoon freshly squeezed lemon juice

1 cup Chicken Stock (page 179)

½ teaspoon finely chopped fresh rosemary

1 teaspoon finely chopped fresh thyme

1 tablespoon chopped fresh flat-leaf parsley

1 tablespoon unsalted cold butter

Kosher salt and freshly ground black pepper

4 slices toasted sourdough bread, for serving

4 tablespoons shaved Parmigiano-Reggiano

I have a number of foragers who bring me mushrooms but two are particularly dear to me, Bob and Alex. Bob is an artist, craftsman, and full-time waiter at Five and Ten, a dear fellow who is blessed with many skill sets, from woodworking to music to foraging and art.

Then there is Alex, whom we named "Wonder Boy" for his outstanding foraging abilities. In 2001, Alex sold the restaurant ten pounds of Clarke County chanterelles that he had foraged in the local woods. He was eleven years old at the time. Over the last nine years, I have probably bought twelve thousand dollars' worth of mushrooms from Wonder Boy at eight dollars a pound.

● ●

Heat your largest fry pan over medium-high heat and when it is hot add the olive oil. Once the olive oil is hot, add the chanterelles. Cook for 4 minutes without moving them around too much.

Add the sherry vinegar and the lemon juice and cook down until fully reduced. Add the stock and reduce by half (you are not exactly reducing so much as hydrating the mushrooms). Add the rosemary, thyme, parsley, and butter. Stir with a wooden spoon to incorporate the butter. Season with salt and pepper.

Evenly spoon the chanterelles over the 4 pieces of toasted bread and garnish with shaved Parmigiano-Reggiano.

SERVES 4

Mushrooms are like sponges full of water. When subjected to heat, they release their liquid, and after some of it evaporates, they will suck the rest back up. So I start by letting them hit the hot oil, sizzle, and then color a bit. Liquid will exude into the pan, partly evaporate, and then return into the mushrooms. Once the pan is pretty much liquid-free we reintroduce flavorful liquids, which the mushrooms will also take up.

These are Bob Fernandez's hands. They are the hands of an artist, musician, forager & great waiter.

These are our chanterelles. They appear after rainy days.

for·age
the act of looking for food or provisions

Duck confit, a self-preserved dish that gains nuance and depth as it ages, will keep in your fridge for up to three months. Make it in advance and this recipe will be a pretty easy "pick up" (restaurant parlance for finishing a dish). If you are having trouble finding rendered duck fat you can order it from D'Artagnan online. I am especially fond of the inexpensive Peking Long Island hybrids commonly available frozen whole.

DUCK CONFIT
with braised
red cabbage &
star anise jus

● ●

In a small bowl, combine the salt, brown sugar, thyme, mustard seeds, peppercorns, and fennel seeds to make a salt-cure mix.

Sprinkle the duck legs with salt cure and place flat on a baking sheet. Cover with plastic wrap and set in the fridge for 24 hours.

Remove the duck from the fridge, rinse off the salt cure, and pat dry.

In a medium pot, melt the duck fat. Add the duck legs, making sure that the fat covers them. Slowly cook on low heat, never boiling the fat. The duck is done when the meat begins to pull back from the drumstick (about 2 hours).

With tongs, pull out the legs and put them into a clean container. Cool the fat to room temperature, then ladle it back over the legs and cover tightly. Put the whole container in the fridge and wait at least 1 or 2 days.

Preheat the oven to 400°F.

When you are hankering for some crisp duck goodness, just take some tongs and dig out the legs, scraping off the excess fat. Place a heavy cast-iron skillet on medium-high heat and add the legs, skin side down. No need for oil. Crisp off for 5 minutes and turn the legs, place the skillet in the oven for 8 minutes, or until the legs are heated through. Remove and serve over braised red cabbage and sauce with 1 tablespoon of star anise jus per duck leg.

SERVES 6

1 cup kosher salt

1 tablespoon lightly packed light brown sugar

2 tablespoons chopped fresh thyme

½ teaspoon mustard seeds

½ teaspoon cracked black peppercorns

½ teaspoon fennel seeds

6 duck legs, trimmed of excess fat

1 quart rendered duck fat

Braised Red Cabbage (recipe follows)

Star Anise Jus (page 79)

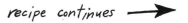

recipe continues ——→

BRAISED RED CABBAGE

MAKES 2 CUPS

1 tablespoon duck fat
¼ cup minced yellow onion
4 cups thinly sliced red cabbage
½ teaspoon salt

¼ cup freshly squeezed orange juice
¼ cup Chicken Stock (page 179)
1 teaspoon cider vinegar
1 bay leaf

In a medium pot with a lid, melt the duck fat over medium heat. Add the onion and sauté for 5 minutes, or until the onion is cooked down. Add the cabbage and stir to wilt. Cook the cabbage down for 5 minutes, add the salt, then add the orange juice, stock, vinegar, and bay leaf. Reduce the heat to a simmer, cover, and cook for 30 minutes (or until tender), stirring occasionally. Discard the bay leaf and serve the cabbage with the duck confit.

STAR ANISE JUS

MAKES ABOUT 1 CUP

2 teaspoons unsalted butter
1 shallot, minced
2 tablespoons cider vinegar
1 tablespoon turbinado sugar
2 tablespoons tawny port

2 whole star anise
1 branch of fresh thyme
1 cup Chicken Stock
   (page 179)
¼ teaspoon kosher salt

Add 1 teaspoon of the unsalted butter to a small saucepan over medium heat. When the butter has melted, add the shallot and cook, stirring occasionally, for 3 minutes. Add the vinegar and sugar and cook until just about dry (be careful not to burn the sugar). Remove from the heat and add the port, star anise, and thyme. Return the pot to the heat and reduce the port by half. Add the stock and reduce by half. Whisk in the remaining teaspoon of butter and simmer over very low heat until ready to serve. Season with the salt to finish.

DUCK CRACKLINGS

MAKES ABOUT ¾ CUP

These are the pork rinds of the fowl world. If you buy a whole duck you will trim a lot of fat and skin, and this is what you do with it. Cracklings become a great garnish for plates as long as you don't eat them all first!

1 cup cut duck fat and skin
   (½-inch squares)

½ teaspoon Maldon sea salt

Place the duck fat and skin in a heavy-bottomed, quart-size pot. Cover with cold water and place on low heat. You are rendering the fat off of the skin and slowly cooking the water away. Stir every 10 minutes or so. It is done after about 2 hours, when the cracklings are crisp and the water has dissipated. Pull out the cracklings with a slotted spoon and place on paper towels. Strain the rendered duck fat into a Mason jar. Save the fat for another culinary occasion. Season the cracklings with the sea salt and store in an airtight container until ready to use.

BRAISED & CRISPED PORK BELLY with CITRUS SALAD

Pork belly is having a heyday, and with good reason. All the kids are cooking it. Nose to tail is great, but a lot of us have been belly gazing. It's a cut that has long been used for bacon but when braised and crisped it takes on a succulence that few can match. It's also inexpensive so you can lavish the table with the best that money can buy, like a beautiful Berkshire or Red Wattle belly, easily obtained online or from a really good grocer or local farmer.

1 pound pork belly, skin removed

1 teaspoon kosher salt

¼ teaspoon freshly ground black pepper

1 tablespoon vegetable oil

½ yellow onion, thinly sliced against the grain

2 sprigs of fresh rosemary

1 garlic clove, smashed

2 cups Chicken Stock (page 179)

3 cups thinly sliced napa cabbage

1 navel orange, cut into supremes (see photo)

1 ruby red grapefruit, cut into supremes

1 tablespoon thinly sliced scallions, white and green parts

2 tablespoons olive oil

2 teaspoons freshly squeezed lemon juice

Preheat the oven to 325°F.

Season the belly with ½ teaspoon of the salt and the pepper. Heat the vegetable oil in a heavy, lidded skillet or Dutch oven that can accommodate the pork belly. When the oil is hot, sear the belly on both sides until nicely browned. Make sure not to crowd the pork belly. Remove the belly and drain off any excess fat.

Make a bed of onion, rosemary, and garlic in the bottom of the pan, add the chicken stock, and bring to a boil. Put the belly back in the pan, cover tightly, and braise in the oven for 2 hours.

Remove the belly from the pan and cool on a plate. Strain the braising liquids through a fine-mesh strainer and place in the fridge. As the braising jus cools, the fat will rise to the top and you can remove the fat by skimming the top with a ladle.

In a medium bowl, toss the cabbage, orange, grapefruit, scallions, olive oil, lemon juice, and the remaining ½ teaspoon of salt. Toss well and set aside.

When the belly is cool enough to handle, divide by cutting into 6 even planks.

Heat a large nonstick pan over medium heat. Crisp the pork belly on both sides and then add the braising jus. Let this cook for 5 minutes and then turn off the heat.

Arrange 6 plates on your counter and place a piece of pork belly on each plate. Place 2 tablespoons of the citrus salad on each piece of belly and then drizzle each with 1 tablespoon of the braising jus.

SERVES 6

In Montreal when the snow melts in the spring, the energy of the people just seems to turn on after the winter doldrums. Ebullience fills the air as the days get longer and everything seems celebrated.

When it comes to the weather I am in a milder state now, and though I miss that ecstatic seasonal change, I have found a yearly phenomenon that fills the void and announces spring with a similar delight . . . ramps.

Ramps are a forager's dream. For a brief stint they are widely available yet fetch a good amount of money at market. They are easy to clean and easy to find in much of the woodsier areas of North America. The bulbs can be had year-round but their true harvest season is when their flat, tender green leaves are about five to eight inches tall, usually in April or early May, depending on where you are. I adore their pungency and turn a deaf ear to those who claim they are too pronounced a taste. To me their wild-leek sweetness with brash garlic undertones is such an addictive taste that I can't get enough. This menu item is perfect for late spring, when okra is rolling in and the ramps are rolling out. Learn to love them.

I have always loved the process of making risotto because it requires patience—a quality that I don't naturally possess. At the restaurant we use Carnaroli rice, similar to Arborio, which results in a creamier risotto with a little more crispness to the center of the grain. I also love the rarer Vialone Nano. The best explanation of judging when a risotto has completed cooking comes from Paul Bertolli in the book *Chez Panisse Cooking,* "There is a point at which risotto is done: when all elements conspire in a union of flavor, texture, and consistency, a timeless moment in cooking, one that can be shared if you serve the dish immediately." In other words, you'll know when it's done!

RISOTTO with OKRA, COUNTRY HAM, BOILED PEANUTS & RAMPS

recipe continues ⟶

4 cups Chicken Stock (page 179)

½ teaspoon salt

3 tablespoons unsalted butter

½ cup minced sweet onion

1 cup Carnaroli or Arborio rice

¼ cup blanched ramps, cut into 1-inch lengths

1 cup okra, tops removed and cut into ½-inch lengths

½ cup shucked Boiled Peanuts (page 56)

1 cup sliced and chopped country ham (thin pieces cut into squares)

2 tablespoons grated Parmigiano-Reggiano

¼ teaspoon kosher salt, or to taste

In a medium saucepan, combine the chicken stock and ¼ teaspoon salt, bring to a simmer, and keep it warm over low heat.

Place a medium saucepan over medium heat. When the pan is warm, add 1 tablespoon of the butter. As soon as the butter begins to bubble and froth, add ¼ cup of the onion and cook, stirring occasionally for 5 minutes, until the onion is soft but not colored.

Add the rice and stir to coat every grain until it's all glistening with butter. After 2 minutes, add 1 cup of the stock and stir with a wooden spoon for 2 minutes. As the stock cooks into the risotto, add more stock 1 cup at a time, stirring a fair bit.

Risotto takes about 17 minutes to cook from when the first stock is introduced to the rice. At the 10-minute mark begin to prepare the rest of the dish, meanwhile keeping a close eye on the risotto and stirring occasionally.

Place a medium fry pan over medium-high heat and add 1 tablespoon of the butter. When the butter bubbles and froths, add the remaining ¼ cup of onion and cook for 5 minutes. Once the onion has developed a lightly golden hue, add the ramps, okra, and boiled peanuts. Cook for 2 minutes, stirring occasionally.

Add 1 tablespoon of the warm stock and the country ham to the onion, ramp, okra, and peanuts. Stir, then add to the risotto. Add the remaining tablespoon of butter and the Parmigiano-Reggiano and stir well. Season to taste with the remaining salt. Serve immediately.

SERVES 6

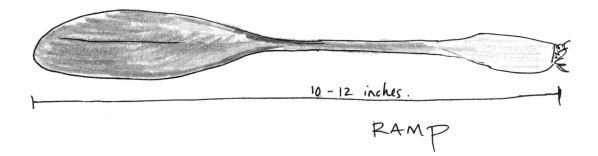

10 - 12 inches.

RAMP

Boiled Peanuts

PARMIGIANO

COUNTRY HAM

ONION

OKRA

RAMPS

RICE   SALT

SOUTHERN CARBONARA

eating well. eating cheap.

Carbonara was my secret weapon when I had a limited food budget in college. It's inexpensive to make and loaded with energy. Now, as a parent, I have also learned that "breakfast noodles" is a pretty easy sell to the kids.

The Southernization of this Italian classic comes in the form of country ham replacing the usual pancetta and a green component in the form of collards. I would love you to use Benton's ham if you can get it (bentonshams.com).

* *

2 tablespoons olive oil

¼ cup minced onion

¼ pound thinly sliced country ham or prosciutto

1 cup finely minced collard greens

½ teaspoon salt

1 pound spaghetti

2 large eggs

¾ cup finely grated Parmigiano-Reggiano

Freshly ground black pepper

2 tablespoons chopped fresh flat-leaf parsley

Place a large pot of water over high heat.

Place a large fry pan over medium heat and add the olive oil. When the oil gets hot add the onion and sweat down until golden, about 3 minutes, then add the country ham and the collard greens. Cook for 2 minutes, stirring occasionally, then turn off the heat.

When the water is rapidly boiling, add the salt and the spaghetti. Stir well and cook the pasta until al dente, usually 9 or 10 minutes. While the pasta is cooking, in a small bowl whisk together the eggs, ½ cup of the Parmigiano-Reggiano, pepper to taste, and the parsley.

Drain the spaghetti in a colander, reserving about ½ cup of the cooking water just to moisten the pasta later if needed. Place the pasta back in the warm pot and add the onion, country ham, and collards. Working quickly, add the egg mixture to the pasta. Stir well with tongs by picking up the pasta and turning and then letting go. You are trying to coat all the pasta with the egg and also tempering the heat by stirring, which will create a custard rather than a scramble. Place in a large bowl to serve at the table and finish with the remaining Parmigiano-Reggiano.

SERVES 4

Bill Neal was the chef of La Residence in Chapel Hill, North Carolina, and later opened Crook's Corner, still a wonderful place under the helm of another Bill, Bill Smith. Neal wrote a great oyster pie recipe that partly inspired this dish. The other inspiration was record-low lobster prices in 2009.

● ●

Preheat the oven to 375°F.

Bring a large pot of water to a vigorous boil over high heat. Season the water with salt and Old Bay.

Remove the elastic bands from the lobster claws. Add the whole lobsters to the pot and cook for 5 minutes in the boiling water, then remove them and shock in ice water to stop the cooking. Using scissors, a mallet, and towels, shell and clean them, reserving the shells for a bisque if you'd like. You should have 2 tails, 4 claws, and the knuckle meat. Coarsely chop all the lobster meat and set aside.

Heat a large fry pan over high heat. Put the olive oil and 1 tablespoon of the butter into the pan. Add the mushrooms and sauté until fully cooked, about 6 minutes, stirring occasionally. Add the sherry vinegar, parsley, and red pepper flakes to the mushrooms, then turn off the heat and set aside.

Heat a small saucepan over medium heat and add 1 tablespoon of the butter. Let the butter bubble and froth and then add the leeks. Add 1 teaspoon water, season with a touch of salt, and cover the pot. Reduce the heat to low and cook until the leeks are tender, about 10 minutes. Add the cream and heat briefly. Season with ¼ teaspoon salt. Place the leek cream in a blender and carefully puree. Set aside.

Butter an 8 by 8-inch baking pan and place ¼ cup of leek cream in the bottom. Arrange 2 toasted boule slices on top of the leek cream, and put a little more cream on top. Layer one third of the lobster meat on top of the bread, then one third of the mushrooms on top of the lobster. Repeat layering the lobster and mushrooms, until all the ingredients have been used. Top with a layer of bread and finish by pouring the remaining leek cream over the pie. Sprinkle with the nutmeg.

Bake for 20 minutes and remove the pan from oven. Cool for 10 minutes and serve.

SERVES 4

Hugh's Lobster Pie

• an homage to Bill Neal •

Kosher salt

1 teaspoon Old Bay seasoning

2 (1-pound) fresh hard-shell Maine lobsters

1 tablespoon extra-virgin olive oil

3 tablespoons unsalted butter

2 cups shiitake mushrooms, sliced

1 tablespoon sherry vinegar

⅓ cup fresh flat-leaf parsley, chopped

Pinch of red pepper flakes

1½ cups minced leeks, white and light-green parts only (see Note page 242)

1 cup heavy cream

8 slices sourdough boule, ⅓-inch thick, drizzled with olive oil, toasted at 375°F until crisp, nicely browned but still with a hint of pliability

Pinch of freshly grated nutmeg

FRIED GREEN TOMATOES
with pickled shrimp and ranch dressing

12 slices green tomato, 1/3 inch thick

1/4 teaspoon kosher salt

1 cup all-purpose flour

3 eggs, beaten with 1/4 cup cold water

1 cup fine yellow cornmeal

1/4 cup bacon fat, lard, or vegetable oil

1/2 cup Ranch Dressing (recipe follows)

12 Pickled Shrimp (page 51), each cut in half lengthwise

12 arugula leaves

This is a great simple recipe for the poster child of Southern cookery, green tomatoes.

Season the green tomato slices with the salt. Set aside. Find three similarly shaped shallow baking dishes and create an assembly line for dredging. In the first dish, place the flour. In the second place the eggs. In the third place the cornmeal. One by one, flour a tomato slice on both sides, then dunk in the egg and dredge in the cornmeal. As you finish each tomato, stack it on a cutting board.

In a large cast-iron skillet, heat the bacon fat over medium heat. In 3 batches of 4 tomatoes per batch, fry the green tomatoes until golden, 2 to 3 minutes per side. Place them on a plate lined with paper towels.

Place 4 plates on the counter and spoon 2 tablespoons of ranch dressing on each one. Put 1 fried green tomato slice down and then place a shrimp on top. Repeat until each plate has 3 slices of green tomato and 3 shrimp. Garnish each plate with 3 arugula leaves and serve immediately.

SERVES 4

RANCH DRESSING

MAKES 1 1/2 CUPS

1/4 cup mayonnaise

1/2 cup buttermilk

1/2 cup crème fraîche

1 tablespoon freshly squeezed lemon juice

1 teaspoon cider vinegar

1 tablespoon finely minced fresh chives

1 teaspoon minced fresh dill

1/2 teaspoon garlic powder

1/8 teaspoon kosher salt

1/8 teaspoon Tabasco sauce

In a small mixing bowl, combine the mayonnaise, buttermilk, crème fraîche, lemon juice, vinegar, chives, dill, garlic powder, salt, and Tabasco. Stir well.

The dressing will stay fresh for 1 week in the fridge.

SHRIMP with celery, caviar, and buttermilk dressing

This is an elegant first course for a summer dinner party. The shrimp is poached and can be served with as much or as little caviar as you'd like (an ounce would be plenty for four people). Pollution and overfishing of wild sturgeon in the Caspian Sea have had devastating effects on caviar production. Up until recently, there was a ban on the import of Russian and Iranian caviars. Although the ban is no longer in effect, we should embrace our own growing industry of sustainable sturgeon farming that is producing world-class caviar. One such program is run by the University of Georgia and makes Sevruga-quality caviar in the North Georgia mountains. It really does par up to some of the best Sevrugas I have tasted.

2 cups Chicken Stock (page 179)

1 cup white wine

1 shallot, minced

2 bay leaves

1 sprig of fresh thyme

Pinch of red pepper flakes

1½ teaspoons kosher salt

2 tablespoons butter

12 American white shrimp (16 to 20 count), head off and peeled

½ cup minced celery

2 tablespoons chopped fresh chives

1 tablespoon Shallot-Thyme Vinaigrette (page 111)

4 tablespoons Buttermilk Dressing (recipe follows)

1 ounce American sturgeon caviar

Combine 1 cup water, the stock, wine, shallot, bay leaves, and thyme in a medium pot, bring to a boil, and reduce to low. Add the red pepper flakes, 1 teaspoon of the salt, and the butter.

Add the shrimp to the poaching liquid and poach for 5 minutes over low heat. Meanwhile, put the celery and chives in a small bowl and lightly dress with the shallot-thyme vinaigrette.

Arrange 4 plates on a counter and place a tablespoon of buttermilk dressing in the center of each. Divide the celery among the 4 plates, cleanly spooning it on top of the buttermilk dressing. Once the 5-minute poaching time has elapsed, remove the shrimp from the poaching liquid and arrange 3 on each plate, on top of the celery. Spoon ¼ ounce of the caviar onto each arrangement of shrimp and serve immediately.

SERVES 4

BUTTERMILK DRESSING

MAKES 1 CUP

½ cup buttermilk
¼ cup crème fraîche
2 tablespoons freshly
  squeezed lemon juice
2 tablespoons cider vinegar

1 tablespoon minced fresh
  chives
1 tablespoon minced fresh
  flat-leaf parsley
Pinch of sea salt
Freshly ground black pepper

In a medium bowl, whisk together the buttermilk with the crème fraîche, lemon juice, cider vinegar, chives, and parsley. Season with sea salt and pepper. Store in a Mason jar for up to 1 week.

YELLOW GRITS
with sauteed shiitakes, fried eggs, and salsa rossa

Tim Mills fashioned his own grist mill from old truck parts and powers it with a strong mule. Because it is made from readily available materials and is inexpensive to build, the mill has been re-created in Africa to crush sorghum. Here in Athens on their small farm ten minutes from downtown, the Millses grind cornmeal, polenta, and grits from organic yellow corn.

½ cup yellow grits

1 teaspoon kosher salt

¼ cup (½ stick) plus 1 tablespoon unsalted butter

8 ounces shiitake mushrooms, stems removed

2 tablespoons Chicken Stock (page 179)

1 tablespoon chopped fresh flat-leaf parsley

4 large eggs

4 tablespoons Salsa Rossa (recipe follows)

Place 2 cups water, the grits, and ½ teaspoon of the salt into a heavy-bottomed saucepan and bring to a boil over medium-high heat. Whisk for a couple of minutes, reduce the heat to low, and switch to a wooden spoon as the grits begin to thicken up. Stir every 5 minutes for about 45 minutes, or until the grits have the consistency of a slightly thinner polenta.

While the grits are cooking, place a large nonstick fry pan over medium-high heat and add 2 tablespoons of the butter. When the butter has melted, add the shiitakes and let cook for 5 minutes, stirring every minute or so. Add the stock and parsley and cook for 2 more minutes. Pour the mushrooms into a small bowl and set aside.

About 10 minutes before the grits are finished cooking, rinse out the large nonstick pan and place it back on medium-low heat. Add 1 tablespoon of the butter to the pan. When the butter bubbles and froths, carefully crack each egg into the pan. Let the eggs cook for 4 minutes, or until the whites are set but the yolks are still brilliantly yellow.

The grits time should be elapsing as the eggs finish. Stir in the remaining 2 tablespoons of butter to finish the grits.

To serve, arrange 4 plates on the counter and divide the cooked grits evenly onto the plates. Arrange the shiitakes on top of the grits and finish the plates with a sunny-side-up egg and a tablespoon of salsa rossa. Eat immediately.

SERVES 4

SALSA ROSSA

MAKES ABOUT 2 CUPS

I have never been to London but I feel like I have a kinship with the River Café, a seminal Italian restaurant there. I remember buying Ruth Rogers and Rose Gray's first cookbook about fifteen years ago and being completely dumbfounded at its simple perfection. The best cookbooks provide a spark for new ideas and this book was like a spark storm to me. I cooked their milk-braised pork loin; we reveled in the freshness of panzanella and adored their simple polentas with roasted mushrooms. Why were the recipes great? Because they were simply written and made use of great-quality ingredients. It is a timeless text and you should get it for your cooking library.

This versatile condiment is lovely on grilled fish or stunning on roasted chicken, and it is delicious as a spread for bread or a sauce for pasta. It's my version of the River Café staple.

1 large red bell pepper
¼ cup plus 2 tablespoons extra-virgin olive oil
6 garlic cloves, peeled and nub end removed
1 shallot, minced
2 ripe roma tomatoes, peeled, seeded, and diced

1 small red jalapeño chile, seeded and minced
1 tablespoon chopped fresh flat-leaf parsley
1 tablespoon chopped fresh basil
¼ teaspoon sea salt

Preheat the oven to 400°F.

Rub the pepper with 1 tablespoon of the olive oil. Roast in the oven on a baking sheet or over the grill until it is well charred. Remove from the heat, place in a bowl, and cover with plastic wrap for 10 minutes. The pepper will still be warm at this point so be careful as you peel, seed, and finely dice. Set aside.

Put the ¼ cup of the olive oil in a small saucepan, then add the whole garlic cloves. Cook over very low heat until tender, about 30 minutes. Remove from the heat and set aside. Once cool, drain the garlic from the oil, saving the oil for another use, such as a vinaigrette.

In a stainless fry pan, warm the remaining tablespoon of olive oil over medium heat. Add the shallot and cook for 2 minutes, then add the tomatoes and roasted pepper. Cook down for 10 minutes and add the poached garlic cloves, the jalapeño chile, parsley, and basil. Season with the salt.

Salsa rossa will stay fresh in the fridge for about 1 week.

Soups and Salads

Great soups blow people away because there is a glut of average soup in the world. Soup should not be a vehicle for resurrecting old and tired vegetables or leftovers from holiday suppers. Please give soup its due respect; making a good one requires skill, persistence, and fresh ingredients. My favorite soups are inspired by standards from American Southern, French, and Italian cooking. Consider serving one of the heartier soups in this chapter as a single-course dinner or one of the chilled soups as part of a light summer supper.

Like soups, salads need not be confined to a supporting role on your menu (especially those with bacon in the list of ingredients!). A few of the salads I make are high in protein and substantial enough to enjoy as a complete meal. Others are refined to just a few ingredients, perfect as starters or finishing courses. The dressing and vinaigrette recipes presented here are key components to their companion salads; however, they were designed to be versatile, so don't hesitate to keep them on hand for everyday use.

Time spent at my family's cottage on Lake Simcoe, just north of Toronto, made me keenly aware of summer vegetables. The cadence created by cucumbers, followed by yellow corn, then bi-colored corn, and finally tomatoes, defined the summer months.

This soup is a beautiful pale yellow and has a natural sweetness that welcomes the vanilla. If lobster is not available, pair with an equally rich shellfish such as shrimp or crawfish.

● ●

Place a large pot of water (about 1 gallon) on the stove for cooking the lobster. Bring the water to a boil and add 1 tablespoon of the kosher salt, all of the Old Bay seasoning, and the lemon. When the water is at a vigorous boil, put in the lobster and cook for 6 minutes. While the lobster is cooking, prepare an ice bath by filling a bowl half with ice and half with water. Remove the lobster from the boiling water and place it in the ice bath to stop the cooking. Once chilled, clean the lobster by breaking off the tail, claws, and knuckles and carefully removing the meat from the shell. Set aside.

In a soup pot with a lid, over medium-high heat, melt the butter. Add the leek and celery and cook until they are soft but not browned, about 3 minutes. Add the corn, bouquet garni, vanilla seeds and pod, and potato. Cook for 2 minutes over medium heat. Add the stock and cover. Continue cooking over medium heat (without boiling) for about 20 minutes, or until the potatoes are tender when poked with a fork.

Add the cream and coconut milk to the soup pot and continue cooking for about 5 minutes. Remove from the heat and puree carefully in a blender. Season with the sea salt.

Chop the lobster into bite-size pieces (this lobster is a garnish and the pieces should not be bigger than what can fit on a spoon) and place in a mixing bowl. Toss the lobster with the tomato, olive oil, and chervil. Divide the lobster equally among 6 soup bowls, then pour soup around it. Serve immediately.

SERVES 6

CORN SOUP
+ VANILLA BEAN
+ COCONUT MILK
+ LOBSTER

1½ tablespoons kosher salt

1 teaspoon Old Bay seasoning

1 slice of fresh lemon

1-pound live fresh Maine lobster

2 tablespoons butter

1 leek, cleaned (see Note page 242) and finely diced

1 celery stalk, finely minced

3 cups fresh corn kernels

Bouquet garni of fresh thyme and bay leaf (see drawing)

½ fresh vanilla bean, scraped seeds and pod

½ cup peeled and 1-inch cubed russet potato

3 cups Chicken Stock (page 179)

¼ cup heavy cream

1 cup coconut milk

1 teaspoon sea salt

1 ripe tomato, diced

1 tablespoon very fruity extra-virgin olive oil

1 tablespoon fresh chervil or dill

THYME

PARSLEY

BAY

bouquet garni

SHE - CRAB SOUP

My in-laws live in Charleston, South Carolina, so I have been fortunate to see the Lowcountry, as the land south of Columbia, South Carolina, is called, and relish in its culinary heritage. One Lowcountry staple is she-crab soup. Silky and smooth with a beautiful uptick of sherry to finish, mine is made in a classic style, using a flour roux as the thickening agent. Typically, I prefer the natural thickening power of potato, rice, or the main vegetable, but in this case, the traditional roux works really well; it's the perfect application for the original light roux, which creates a silky but not chalky finish on the palate.

2 tablespoons unsalted butter

2 tablespoons all-purpose flour

1 cup minced yellow onion

⅓ cup minced celery

2 garlic cloves, minced

½ teaspoon kosher salt, plus more to taste

¼ teaspoon freshly ground black pepper, plus more to taste

¼ teaspoon ground mace

2 cups whole milk

1 cup Chicken Stock (page 179)

¼ cup heavy cream

1 tablespoon Louisiana-style hot sauce, such as Louisiana Hot Sauce or Texas Pete

½ tablespoon Worcestershire sauce

2 cups fresh blue crab, picked through and chopped

2 hard-boiled eggs, chopped

¼ cup minced scallions, white and green parts

1 teaspoon smoked paprika

Fino sherry

Melt the butter in a medium-size soup pot over medium heat. When the butter bubbles and froths, whisk in the flour and cook for 5 minutes, stirring often with a wooden spoon. The color will have gone from white to blonde. You now have a blonde roux. Stir in the onion and celery and cook for 5 minutes. Add the garlic, salt, pepper, and mace, and cook for 1 minute. Add the milk, stock, cream, hot sauce, and Worcestershire sauce. Reduce the heat and simmer for 15 minutes. Season with salt and pepper. Add the crab and simmer for another 20 minutes.

Pour the soup into 6 bowls and garnish with the hard-boiled egg, scallions, and a pinch of smoked paprika. Serve with a shot of fino sherry, which can be poured into the soup or sipped on the side.

SERVES 6

Mace is nutmeg's gentler younger sibling. It's actually ground from the outer membrane of the nutmeg seed.

This soup reminds me of Banff, Alberta, where I lived when I was a spritely young cook at the Alpenglow Café in the Banff Youth Hostel. Though an idyllic setting, the food program was not challenging. Grilled cheeses and French fries were popular menu items, but I loved making a version of a *Moosewood Cookbook* mushroom soup as a special. It introduced me to the classic flavor affinity of mushrooms and sherry. I still love the combination.

CHANTERELLE SOUP
with almonds & sherry

Melt the butter in a large heavy-bottomed soup pot set over medium-high heat. When the butter starts to bubble and froth, add the onion and celery. Sweat down for 5 minutes and then add the mushrooms. Raise the heat to high and cook for 10 minutes, stirring occasionally.

Add the bouquet garni to the pot. Then add the potato, salt, and 3 cups of the stock. Reduce the heat and simmer for about 25 minutes, or until the potatoes are tender.

Add the cream to the pot and cook for 2 minutes. Remove from the heat, discard the bouquet garni, and puree the soup, in batches, in a blender, taking care not to fill the blender too full. If the soup is too thick, thin with the remaining stock.

Place the almonds in a sealable plastic bag and lightly crush them with the bottom of a fry pan.

Pour the soup into 6 bowls, pour a shot of sherry into each bowl, and sprinkle with the almonds.

SERVES 6

1 tablespoon unsalted butter

1 medium yellow onion, minced

2 celery stalks, peeled and minced

2 cups chanterelles, cleaned and finely chopped

Small bouquet garni of fresh thyme, 2 fresh parsley sprigs, and 2 bay leaves (see drawing on page 99)

1 medium russet potato, peeled and cut into 1-inch dice

½ teaspoon salt

3½ cups Chicken Stock (page 179)

½ cup heavy cream

2 tablespoons toasted almonds, slivered

½ cup fino sherry

Commonly used in Southern cooking, a ham hock is a cross-cut piece of the shank that provides foundational flavor. In this recipe, the smoked ham hock should be fairly meaty. If you get freshly dried black-eyed peas, they should plump up nicely without soaking.

● ●

Place a 4- to 6-quart soup pot over medium heat and add the butter. When the butter is melted, add the onion, carrot, and celery and cook for 10 minutes, stirring occasionally.

Add the garlic, black-eyed peas, chicken stock, and ham hock. Cook until the peas are tender, about 1 hour. Skim to remove the airy white bean matter that floats to the top.

While the soup is cooking, cut the cornbread into ½ by ½-inch cubes. In a large cast-iron skillet over medium heat, toast the cubed cornbread in the bacon fat until crisp. If necessary, cook the croutons in batches, making sure to toast all sides. Cool on a large plate.

Remove the ham hock from the soup pot, cool, and take the meat off the bone. Coarsely chop the meat and return it to the pot. Discard the bone and any connective tissue.

Add the thyme, mustard greens, tomato, and salt to the soup. Cook for 10 more minutes and then portion into bowls for serving. Drizzle each bowl with a couple drops of cider vinegar and a dash of olive oil, garnish with the cornbread croutons, and serve immediately.

SERVES 6 WITH LEFTOVERS

FIELD PEA, HAM HOCK & MUSTARD GREEN SOUP WITH CORNBREAD CROUTONS

1 tablespoon unsalted butter

½ cup minced sweet onion

½ cup diced carrot

1 celery stalk, minced

3 garlic cloves, peeled

½ cup dried black-eyed peas

6 cups Chicken Stock (page 179) or low-sodium chicken broth

1 smoked ham hock, about 1 pound

2 cups cubed Cornbread (recipe follows)

2 tablespoons bacon fat

1 tablespoon chopped fresh thyme

2 cups chopped mustard greens

1 cup chopped tomato

1 teaspoon kosher salt

1 tablespoon cider vinegar

Extra-virgin olive oil

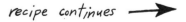

recipe continues ⟶

CORNBREAD

SERVES 8

Cornbread should not have sugar in it. That's cake. As for what you put on cornbread after it's done, that's up to you. Sorghum butter is a nice touch, but so is unsalted butter.

2 cups white cornmeal
½ cup all-purpose flour
1 teaspoon baking powder
1 teaspoon baking soda
½ teaspoon kosher salt

¾ cup whole milk
¾ cup buttermilk
1 large egg
¼ cup bacon fat

Preheat the oven to 425°F.

In a large bowl, mix together the cornmeal, flour, baking powder, baking soda, and salt. In a separate bowl, mix together the milk, buttermilk, and egg. Add the wet mixture to the dry mixture. Stir well to combine.

Heat a 10-inch cast-iron skillet over medium heat and add the bacon fat. When the fat is hot (not smoking), add it to the batter and stir. Pour the batter into the cast-iron skillet and place in the oven. Bake for 20 minutes.

Remove the cornbread from the oven and let it cool slightly in the cast-iron skillet, for 15 to 20 minutes. Turn the cornbread over onto a cutting board. Cool completely, then cut into wedges to serve.

roasted CAULIFLOWER soup with brown butter, breadcrumbs, capers and dilled whipped cream

When I say cauliflower florets, I do not mean those bags of precut vegetables that are becoming commonplace at the grocery store. Buy a whole head and use a knife!

I like my soups to be thin, but the consistency can vary as long as it never verges on gruel or pap. Pureed soups should be silky and smooth, creamy and refreshing. This is a simple pureed soup that showcases the often misunderstood cauliflower—misunderstood, that is, until the mid-eighties, when roasting it revealed its ability to caramelize, which gives it a more complex, nutty flavor.

* *

3 cups cauliflower florets

1 tablespoon olive oil

2 tablespoons unsalted butter

½ medium yellow onion, minced

1 leek, cleaned (see Note page 242), dark green discarded and the rest finely sliced against the grain

1 celery stalk, peeled and diced

Small bouquet garni of fresh thyme, bay leaf, and fresh parsley sprigs (see drawing, page 99)

2 cups Chicken Stock (page 179)

1¼ teaspoons kosher salt

1¼ cups heavy cream

¼ teaspoon grated lemon zest

¼ cup bread crumbs (page 228)

2 tablespoons chopped fresh dill

2 teaspoons capers, chopped

Preheat the oven to 425°F.

Toss the cauliflower with the olive oil, place the florets on a rimmed roasting pan, and roast in the oven until they are nicely browned, about 15 minutes. Set aside.

In a large soup pot, melt 1 tablespoon of the butter over medium heat. Add the onion, leek, and celery. Sweat until translucent, about 5 minutes. Add the roasted cauliflower, bouquet garni, and chicken stock. Bring to a boil, then simmer for 15 minutes.

Season with 1 teaspoon of the salt, then add 1 cup of the heavy cream and the lemon zest. Puree the soup in a blender and then pass through a strainer.

Melt the remaining 1 tablespoon of butter in a small skillet over medium heat until it browns slightly. Add the bread crumbs and toss the pan to get the bread crumbs toasting. Once they have a nice sheen and are well toasted (but not burnt), pour the bread crumbs onto a large plate to cool.

Whisk the remaining ¼ cup of cream in a bowl to soft peaks and fold in the dill and the remaining ¼ teaspoon of salt.

Reheat the soup if necessary and serve in bowls. Top each with a spoonful of whipped cream and sprinkle the bread crumbs and capers on top.

SERVES 6

This soup originated from some work I did for the National Peanut Board, which led to my researching South Carolina Lowcountry food and the popularity of peanuts in Gullah cuisine. When I finally wrote down the recipe, I was struck by how odd it looked on paper but how good the results were.

PEANUT SOUP with AVOCADO

In a heavy-bottomed soup pot, melt the butter over medium heat until it just begins to bubble and froth. Add the onion and celery and sweat down for about 5 minutes, stirring occasionally.

Add the tomato, curry powder, and chipotle. Stir and cook through to develop the flavors for about 2 minutes. Add the sweet potato, peanut butter, and stock. Raise the heat to medium-high and bring the soup to a boil. Once the boil has been reached, reduce to a simmer for 15 minutes, or until the sweet potato is tender. Add the cream. Remove from the heat.

Puree the soup while still warm in batches in a blender, taking care not to overfill the blender. Then pass it through a fine-mesh strainer and season to taste with sea salt and black pepper.

Cut the avocado in half and remove the pit. Sprinkle with the lime juice and season with kosher salt.

When you are ready to serve the soup, place it back in a clean pot and reheat. Portion it into 6 bowls and garnish each with a scoop of avocado and a few chopped peanuts.

SERVES 6

1 tablespoon unsalted butter

½ cup minced yellow onion

½ cup minced celery

1 cup diced tomato

1 tablespoon curry powder

1 tablespoon chopped chipotle in adobo

1 medium sweet potato, peeled and cubed to 1 inch

½ cup smooth, unsweetened, all-natural peanut butter

4 cups Chicken Stock (page 179)

1 tablespoon heavy cream

Pinch of sea salt

Freshly ground black pepper

1 ripe avocado

1 teaspoon freshly squeezed lime juice

Pinch of kosher salt

2 tablespoons chopped roasted peanuts

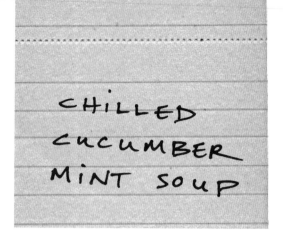

CHILLED CUCUMBER MINT SOUP

Mint and cucumber are two things that you should never have to buy if you have a backyard in most climates in the United States. They grow like weeds. The problem quickly becomes how to use the bounty. This is one answer. It's a refreshing soup that takes about ten minutes to make. If you want to make more of a meal out of this dish you could garnish it with poached chicken or shrimp.

1 tablespoon plus ½ teaspoon olive oil

1 leek (white and light-green parts), cleaned (see Note page 242) and cut into small dice

1 celery stalk, minced

3 cups peeled, seeded, and diced cucumbers

1 teaspoon toasted fennel seeds, ground

2 cups low-fat plain yogurt

2 tablespoons fresh mint leaves

½ teaspoon grated lemon zest

2 tablespoons freshly squeezed lemon juice

½ teaspoon honey

Pinch of cayenne

¼ teaspoon salt

Warm a large fry pan over medium heat and add 1 tablespoon of olive oil. When the oil is warm, add the leeks and cook for 5 minutes. Add the celery and cook for an additional 3 minutes. Remove from the heat and set aside to cool.

Place the cucumbers in a blender and add the cooked leeks and celery, the fennel seeds, yogurt, mint, lemon zest, lemon juice, honey, and cayenne. Blend until smooth. If the soup is too thick, thin it down with water while the blender is running. Season with salt, then refrigerate for 1 hour, or until thoroughly chilled.

To serve, pour 1 cup of soup into each bowl and garnish with a drizzle of the remaining olive oil.

SERVES 6

mint   cucumber

In July, when the tomatoes and basil are in full force, make this simple salad with burrata, a soft Italian cheese made from a mozzarella skin filled with a mixture of cream and mozzarella. Years ago, I tried some burrata in the kitchen of Babbo (Mario Batali's seminal New York restaurant) and I recall thinking it was the best thing ever.

Di Stefano and Gioia are two California artisan producers making quality burrata, and its availability is beginning to grow. If you can't find burrata, use a high-quality fresh mozzarella.

TOMATO SALAD with BURRATA, BASIL & CHOPPED OLIVES

Core the tomatoes, slice into ½-inch-thick slices, and place in a large bowl. Season them evenly with the salt, drizzle with the olive oil and vinegar, and gently toss to coat.

Cut the burrata into 8 pieces (about ¼ inch thick) and set aside.

Arrange 4 plates on your counter. Place 2 pieces of burrata on each plate and evenly arrange the tomatoes and basil on top. Spoon 1 tablespoon of the olives on each tomato stack. Serve immediately.

SERVES 4

2 pounds heirloom tomatoes

½ teaspoon kosher salt

2 tablespoons extra-virgin olive oil

1 tablespoon sherry vinegar

½ pound burrata or fresh mozzarella

16 fresh basil leaves

¼ cup pitted and coarsely chopped kalamata olives

DO NOT STORE TOMATOES IN FRIDGE. thanks Ant

SPINACH SALAD with spicy pecans, blue cheese, and pear, with shallot-thyme vinaigrette

1 tablespoon unsalted butter

1 cup pecan halves

½ teaspoon granulated sugar

½ teaspoon kosher salt

Pinch of cayenne

1 pound baby spinach leaves, stems removed

4 tablespoons Shallot-Thyme Vinaigrette (recipe follows)

½ cup blue cheese (such as Asher Blue, Maytag, Stilton, or Bleu d'Auvergne), crumbled

1 pear, halved and cored (unpeeled)

To me, great Stilton, such as Colston Bassett, is at the top of all things blue and stinky. But it does face some fierce competition: Sweetgrass Dairy in Thomasville, Georgia, makes a Stilton imposter, an absolute stunner called Asher Blue.

This salad has been on Five and Ten's menu for ten years because I fear an uprising should I remove it. It's the way the spinach wilts under the vinaigrette and the cheese softens, together with the crispness of the pear and the crunchiness of the nuts; it all comes together to be quite a spectacular salad, one that is easy to assemble.

The shallot-thyme vinaigrette is the restaurant's workhorse vinaigrette. It is always in the fridge and should always be in yours, too. For best results, prepare it twenty-four hours in advance to allow the flavors to develop.

Place a heavy fry pan over medium heat and add the butter to the pan. When the butter bubbles and froths, add the pecans and toast lightly, stirring often. Add the sugar and ¼ teaspoon of the salt and toss to coat. Sprinkle the cayenne over the nuts. When they are nice and toasted, remove the nuts to a plate to cool.

Place the spinach in a large salad bowl and season with the remaining ¼ teaspoon of salt. Add the vinaigrette, blue cheese, and the pecans. Toss well. Slice the pear, add to the salad, and serve immediately.

SERVES 4

SHALLOT-THYME VINAIGRETTE

MAKES 4 CUPS

6 stems (about ½ ounce) of fresh thyme
3 shallots, finely minced
⅓ cup freshly squeezed lemon juice
⅔ cup champagne vinegar
3 cups extra-virgin olive oil
½ teaspoon dry mustard
½ teaspoon kosher salt

Using the blunt side of a large, heavy kitchen knife, bruise the thyme by pounding it about 10 times to extract its essential oils.

Place the shallots, thyme, lemon juice, champagne vinegar, olive oil, dry mustard, and salt in a quart-size Mason jar. Close tightly and store in the refrigerator for 24 hours.

Remove the vinaigrette from the fridge, bring to room temperature, and pass through a conical strainer, pressing the solids vigorously with a tamper or small ladle to extract the thyme and shallot flavors. Discard the solids and place the vinaigrette back into the quart jar and seal tightly. Shake well before using.

Conical strainers, commonly used in traditional French cooking to make smoother vinaigrettes & sauces, can withstand repeated pressure better than a round strainer can. You could also use a food mill as an alternative.

ROASTED CARROT & BEET SALAD with FETA, PULLED PARSLEY & CUMIN VINAIGRETTE

1 teaspoon salt

1 pound baby carrots, peeled, ½ inch of green top left on

1 pound baby beets, cleaned but not peeled

¼ pound feta

1 tablespoon extra-virgin olive oil

¼ cup **Cumin Vinaigrette** (recipe follows)

1 cup pulled fresh flat-leaf parsley leaves

The beautiful beets and carrots harvested at the same time in the early fall by our local farm supplier inspired this recipe.

Feta is a brined sheep's-milk or cow's-milk cheese made in many places, but the European Union recently mandated that only feta from Greece can be called "feta" so we'll start to see a bunch of "Greek-Style Salad Cheeses" in grocery stores. My favorite feta, Valbreso, is from France, is 100 percent sheep's milk, and is for sale at Kroger in Athens, Georgia. If I can get it in Athens, chances are good your neighborhood grocer has it. If you live in a very isolated place, then order your feta from Amazon.com.

Vinaigrettes need balance and should be made with the other salad components in mind. If you are dressing salty feta, scale back on the salt content in the dressing.

* *

Preheat the oven to 450°F.

Bring a large pot of water to a vigorous boil, add ½ teaspoon of the salt, then add the carrots. Blanch for 1 minute and remove to a bowl of ice water to stop the cooking. Once cool, remove and set aside.

Place the beets in a large pot of cold water. Bring to a boil, add the remaining ½ teaspoon of salt, and simmer until the beets are tender. Strain the beets and peel them using paper towels to rub off the skin. This is easier when they are still warm.

Crumble the feta and set aside.

Toss the carrots with ½ tablespoon of the olive oil and place them on half of a rimmed baking sheet. Toss the beets with the remaining olive oil and place on the other half of the baking sheet. Roast for 15 minutes.

Remove the beets and carrots from the oven and place in separate bowls. Add 1 tablespoon of the vinaigrette and ½ cup of the parsley to the beets and toss. Add 1 tablespoon of the vinaigrette, the remaining parsley, and the feta to the carrots and toss. Divide the carrots evenly among 6 plates. Then divide the beets evenly among the plates and gently mix with the carrots. Drizzle with a touch more of the vinaigrette.

SERVES 6

recipe continues ⟶

CUMIN VINAIGRETTE

MAKES ¾ CUP

1 teaspoon Dijon mustard
½ cup extra-virgin olive oil
1 teaspoon freshly squeezed
    lemon juice
2 teaspoons sherry vinegar
1 teaspoon cumin seeds,
    toasted in a dry pan and then
    pulverized

1 tablespoon finely chopped
    fresh mint
Salt and freshly ground black
    pepper

Place the Dijon mustard in a bowl and whisk in the olive oil, then the lemon juice and the sherry vinegar. Add the cumin and the mint. Season with salt and pepper to taste. The vinaigrette will last for 10 days in the fridge.

An Ode to Carrots:

I eat many pounds of carrots throughout the week. They are my snack food. My palate has become quite particular about them, and when the season breaks for local carrots I become quite a glutton. The great thing about carrots around here is that they have two harvest times, one in early spring (the bounty of a late fall planting) and then one in early summer (from a spring seeding). Our local farmers grow the most beautiful carrot varieties, from the almost straight-legged NANTES to the classic IMPERATOR to the golf-ball-shaped PARISIANS to Wonka-esque COSMIC PURPLES to the anvil-shaped CHANTENAYS. The crisp sweetness of local carrots is unrivaled and you should hunt some down at your farmer's market or grow them yourselves!

Folks who generally don't like okra (yet another under-appreciated vegetable) actually love fried okra. I often think about texture and the role it plays in salads. In this case, the crunch of the fried okra replaces that of the crouton.

You really want to hunt for smaller okra pods, which will be less wooden than some of the bigger ones. Look for pods that are bright in color, firm, and blemish free.

* *

Core the tomatoes and dice to about 1 inch. Place them in a large salad bowl and season with ½ teaspoon of the salt. Add the cucumber and toss lightly. Add the arugula and Parmigiano-Reggiano and set aside.

Prep the okra by tossing it in a small bowl with the buttermilk. Place the cornmeal in an 8 by 10-inch or 8 by 12-inch baking dish and season with the remaining teaspoon of salt. Lift the okra out of the buttermilk and dredge into the cornmeal and then set aside on a rimmed baking sheet.

Place a large, heavy cast-iron pan over high heat and add the vegetable oil. Bring the oil up to 325°F and carefully add the okra to the oil. Fry for about 5 minutes or until the okra are crisp and golden, turning them with tongs to ensure even goldenness. Remove them from the pan with a slotted spoon and rest on a slotted rack set over a baking sheet.

Once the okra has cooled, add it to the salad bowl. Add the Shallot-Thyme Vinaigrette and toss gently.

Pour ¼ cup of the green goddess dressing onto a large platter. With the back of a spoon, smooth it out and arrange the salad on top of the dressing.

SERVES 6

fried okra salad with heirloom tomatoes, arugula, and green goddess dressing

- 2 pounds heirloom tomatoes
- 1½ teaspoons kosher salt
- 1 small cucumber, peeled and sliced in ¼-inch rounds (1 cup)
- 1 cup baby arugula leaves
- ½ cup shaved Parmigiano-Reggiano
- 2 cups okra, cut into 1-inch lengths
- ½ cup buttermilk
- 2 cups white cornmeal
- 1 cup vegetable oil
- 2 tablespoons Shallot-Thyme Vinaigrette (page 111)
- ¼ cup Green Goddess Dressing (recipe follows)

recipe continues ⟶

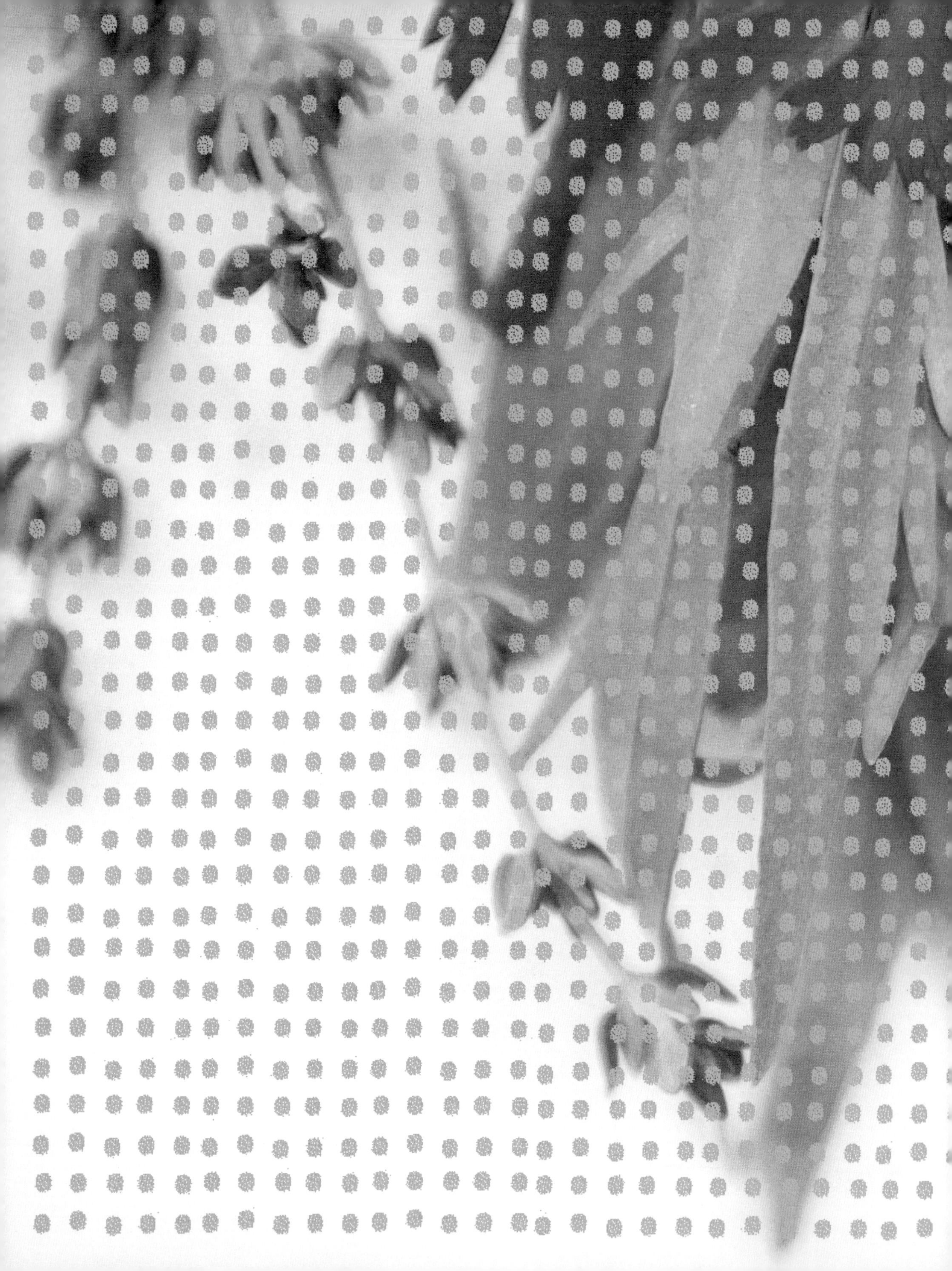

GREEN GODDESS DRESSING

MAKES 1½ CUPS

1 teaspoon regular (not salt-packed or marinated) anchovies, rinsed and chopped

¼ cup chopped fresh flat-leaf parsley

1 tablespoon chopped fresh chives

1 teaspoon chopped fresh tarragon

1 teaspoon chopped fresh thyme

½ cup mayonnaise

¼ cup crème fraîche (or whole-milk yogurt)

1 tablespoon champagne vinegar

1 teaspoon freshly squeezed lemon juice

¼ teaspoon kosher salt

Freshly ground black pepper

Place the anchovies, parsley, chives, tarragon, thyme, mayonnaise, crème fraîche, champagne vinegar, lemon juice, salt, and pepper to taste in a food processor. Process for about 10 seconds until smooth and green. Taste and correct the seasoning. Thin with a little water if necessary.

FAVA BEANS with mint, prosciutto, Parmigiano-Reggiano, & brown butter vinaigrette

Fava beans are the bane of my kitchen staff's existence because they are labor-intensive legumes. First, you have to shell the large pod, then blanch the beans, shock them in ice water, and, finally, peel the tough skin off of each bean to reveal the bright green goodness within. When the fava season begins in April, I get excited and order case upon case, resulting in a great amount of tedious, repetitious work. One dish person, into her third case of beautiful favas, suddenly blurted out in a Darth Vader voice, "Luke, I am your Fava."

2 cups shelled fava beans, blanched for 1 minute and then peeled

½ cup fresh mint leaves

1 cup arugula leaves

8 tablespoons Brown Butter Vinaigrette (recipe follows)

Kosher salt and freshly ground black pepper

8 thin slices of prosciutto (about 1 ounce each)

¼ pound Parmigiano-Reggiano, shaved with a peeler to thin strips

Combine the fava beans, mint, and arugula in a medium bowl and dress with a tablespoon of the vinaigrette. Season with salt and pepper.

Place 1 slice of prosciutto on each of 4 plates and then divide the favas equally among the plates. Arrange shavings of cheese over each plate and then top with another slice of prosciutto. Drizzle each plate with 1 teaspoon of the remaining vinaigrette around the plate.

SERVES 4

BROWN BUTTER VINAIGRETTE

MAKES 1 CUP

4 tablespoons (½ stick) unsalted butter

1 shallot, minced

¼ teaspoon kosher salt

Freshly ground black pepper

3 tablespoons sherry vinegar

½ cup extra-virgin olive oil

1 teaspoon finely chopped fresh thyme

1 tablespoon finely chopped fresh flat-leaf parsley

Place the butter in a medium saucepan over medium heat. Keep an eye on it because you are looking to brown the milk solids, not burn them. When the butter is a nutty brown color, turn off the heat and add the shallot, salt, and pepper to taste. The shallot will cook as the butter cools. Pour the brown butter mixture into a blender and add the vinegar.

Turn the blender on medium and slowly drizzle in the olive oil. Turn off the blender; adjust with salt and pepper, if needed. Add the thyme and parsley, and stir to combine. This vinaigrette will last for 1 week in the fridge.

LOCAL LETTUCES
with FETA, RADISHES, and DILL PICKLE VINAIGRETTE.

The lettuces I am thinking of are the ones that appear at our farmer's markets when the weather starts to chill in the fall and then when it warms from winter again: the lolla rossa, the baby gems, the tango leaves, and the red and green oak leaf. All these lettuces need is a little feta and a simple vinaigrette.

This vinaigrette is a flavor ode to where I am from and the wonderfully odd dill pickle–flavored potato chips of my youth. Their popularity never migrated south. In the South, pickles take another strange turn into weirdness in the form of Mississippi Delta Koolickles: large whole dill pickles marinated in Kool-Aid. Not for me, but I am working on some ideas. Little gherkins marinated in vermouth and fresh herbs would be great in a cocktail.

1 pound small lettuces, cleaned and cut to bite size

⅛ teaspoon kosher salt

⅓ cup Dill Pickle Vinaigrette (recipe follows)

12 radishes, thinly sliced

¼ cup feta, crumbled

Place the lettuces in a large salad bowl and sprinkle with the salt. Add the vinaigrette and toss well with your hands. Add the radishes and feta and toss again. Serve immediately.

SERVES 6

DILL PICKLE VINAIGRETTE

MAKES 1 CUP

1 shallot, minced

1 teaspoon Dijon mustard

⅓ cup chopped dill pickle

2 tablespoons cider vinegar

½ cup extra-virgin olive oil

2 tablespoons chopped fresh dill

⅛ teaspoon kosher salt

Make the vinaigrette by adding the shallot, mustard, pickle, and vinegar to a blender. Blend on low speed. As soon as the pickle is pureed, add the olive oil in a slow stream. Once all of the oil has been incorporated, turn off the blender, then stir in the dill and salt. Pour the vinaigrette into a quart-size Mason jar and set aside. Any extra dressing will stay fresh for a good 10 days in the fridge.

Brussels sprouts get a bad name. Most of the bad rap comes from the fact that so many of us were forced to eat drastically overcooked, mushy, under-seasoned Brussels sprouts when we were kids. This recipe will open your eyes to the wonderful side of a much-maligned vegetable. You won't have to hide them in your napkin ever again.

● ● ●● ● ● ● ● ● ● ●● ● ●● ● ●● ● ● ●● ● ● ●

In a medium salad bowl, toss the Brussels sprouts, pecans, cheese, and parsley. Add the vinaigrette, toss, season, and plate.

SERVES 6

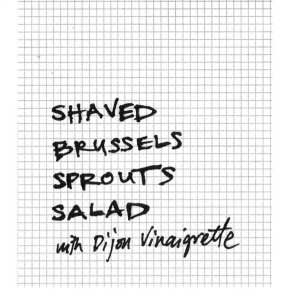

SHAVED
BRUSSELS
SPROUTS
SALAD
with Dijon Vinaigrette

1 quart Brussels sprouts, thinly shaved by hand or on a small mandoline

1 cup roasted pecan halves, slightly broken up

1 cup shaved Pecorino Romano cheese (or Parmigiano-Reggiano)

½ cup pulled fresh flat-leaf parsley leaves, lightly chopped

¼ cup Dijon Vinaigrette (recipe follows)

Kosher salt and freshly ground black pepper

recipe continues →

1 teaspoon Dijon mustard
3 tablespoons extra virgin olive oil
1 tablespoon freshly squeezed lemon juice
1 teaspoon sherry vinegar
kosher salt and freshly ground black pepper
1 tablespoon finely chopped fresh flat-leaf parsley

DIJON VINAIGRETTE

MAKES ½ CUP

Put the mustard in a small heavy bowl that won't move around when you start whisking. Slowly whisk in the olive oil to emulsify. If it gets too thick, dilute with a touch of water. Once the oil is incorporated, add the lemon juice and vinegar, season with salt and pepper to taste, and finish with the parsley.

WATERMELON SALAD WITH FETA, ARUGULA & SERRANO CHILE VINAIGRETTE

6 tablespoons Serrano Chile Vinaigrette (recipe follows)

1 medium seedless watermelon, skin and rind removed, cut into ¾-inch-thick by 3 by 3-inch squares (16 squares)

1 serrano chile, thinly sliced

¼ pound baby arugula leaves

½ teaspoon kosher salt

½ pound feta, cut into 16 slices (¼ inch thick)

Watermelons are a summer mainstay in the South and should be more than dessert. This idea came from watching Latinos in various kitchens sprinkle mango with red pepper flakes or cayenne. Sweet and hot!

Shake the vinaigrette vigorously. Place the watermelon squares, serrano slices, and arugula in a large bowl, and dress with half of the vinaigrette. Season lightly with salt.

Place 4 plates on a counter. Add a small amount of dressed arugula on each plate, then 1 slice of watermelon, then 1 slice of feta. Repeat until each plate has 4 slices of watermelon and 4 slices of feta. Garnish with the dressed serrano slices and then drizzle a touch of the vinaigrette around each plate. Serve immediately.

SERVES 4

recipe continues ⟶

SERRANO CHILE VINAIGRETTE

MAKES 1 CUP

½ cup olive oil
1 tablespoon freshly squeezed
  lime juice
1 tablespoon champagne
  vinegar

1 shallot, minced
1 serrano chile, thinly sliced
½ tablespoon chopped fresh
  thyme
¼ teaspoon kosher salt

Combine the olive oil, lime juice, champagne vinegar, shallot, chile, thyme, and salt in a Mason jar, tighten the lid, and shake vigorously. This vinaigrette will last for 10 days in the fridge and will increase in heat as it sits.

this is a picture of Serrano Chile Vinaigrette

The key to this salad is the vinaigrette. When you put the egg on this salad you need a vinaigrette that has enough acid to deal with it. You must have that puckery bite or it becomes too leaden.

* *

Lyonnaise SALAD WITH BACON VINAIGRETTE

In a large bowl, combine the frisée, sliced apples, and parsley.

Place the bacon vinaigrette in a small pot and warm over medium heat for 2 minutes.

Season the salad with the pinch of salt and dress with ¼ cup of the warm vinaigrette. Toss well and then split equally among 6 plates.

Place a wide, shallow pot on the stove on medium-high heat and fill 2 inches with water. Bring to a boil, then simmer over low heat. Add the vinegar and the teaspoon of salt to the water. Crack the eggs individually into 6 small bowls and then carefully pour each egg into the water. Poach the eggs for 3 to 4 minutes depending on how soft you like your yolks. I like mine quite soft. Remove the eggs from the water with a slotted spoon, dabbing the bottom of the spoon onto a kitchen towel to remove any excess moisture, and place a poached egg on top of each salad. Finish each plate with a drizzle (about a tablespoon each) of the bacon vinaigrette.

SERVES 6

2 heads of frisée lettuce, cleaned and outer darker green leaves removed

2 red apples, thinly sliced

½ cup fresh flat-leaf parsley leaves

1 cup Bacon Vinaigrette (recipe follows)

1 teaspoon plus a pinch of kosher salt

1 tablespoon white vinegar

6 large eggs

BACON VINAIGRETTE

MAKES 2 CUPS

¼ pound bacon, finely diced
1 tablespoon grain mustard
½ cup olive oil
¼ cup sherry vinegar

1 tablespoon freshly squeezed lemon juice
2 tablespoons chopped fresh flat-leaf parsley
Pinch of kosher salt

In a large skillet over medium heat, cook the bacon until crisp but not burnt, then remove it from the pan using a slotted spoon. Set the bacon strips, side by side, on some paper towels. Turn off the heat but save 2 tablespoons of the warm rendered bacon fat.

Place a medium bowl on a damp kitchen towel. Add the mustard and slowly whisk in the olive oil. Once the oil is incorporated, add the warm bacon fat, sherry vinegar, lemon juice, parsley, and the bacon. Stir well and season with salt. Heat gently to serve. This vinaigrette will last for 1 week in the fridge.

B.L.T.
SALAD
with boiled dressing

½ teaspoon olive oil

4 slabs of bacon (each about 2 ounces,
    5 inches long by 2 inches wide by
    ½ inch thick)

1 cup Chicken Stock (page 179)

1 ripe avocado

½ cup Boiled Dressing (recipe follows)

2 cups torn butter lettuce leaves

8 Roasted Tomatoes (recipe follows)

1 teaspoon freshly squeezed lemon
    juice

1 tablespoon olive oil

¼ teaspoon kosher salt

4 slices of brioche or challah (each
    about 1 inch thick), buttered and
    lightly toasted in the oven under
    low broil

The dressing on this salad is a step away from the mayonnaise that usually hangs with the trilogy, but don't be scared. It's a really old-school dressing and should be part of your repertoire.

Warm a heavy pot that will comfortably fit all your bacon slices over medium heat. Add the olive oil, then the bacon. Gently crisp the bacon over medium heat for 4 minutes. Flip the bacon and crisp for another 4 minutes.

Turn off the heat (for safety purposes), then add the chicken stock. It will splatter a bit, so be careful. Cover and turn the heat back on low. Braise for 20 minutes and set aside.

Pit, peel, and slice the avocado into ¼-inch-thick slices. Set aside.

Spread 2 tablespoons of boiled dressing on each of the 4 plates. In a large bowl, combine the lettuce, tomatoes, bacon, and avocado slices. Add the lemon juice and olive oil and gently toss. Season with salt. Arrange the salad carefully over the boiled dressing, distributing all ingredients evenly. Lean a slice of buttered toasted brioche next to each salad.

SERVES 4

ROASTED TOMATOES

4 ripe roma tomatoes
½ teaspoon chopped fresh
    thyme
¼ teaspoon kosher salt

¼ teaspoon freshly ground
    black pepper
1 teaspoon olive oil

Preheat the oven to 275°F.

Halve the tomatoes by slicing them from pole to pole. Place the tomatoes in a small bowl and season with the thyme, salt, and pepper. Drizzle with the olive oil, and combine.

Place the tomatoes on a rimmed baking sheet and bake for 1 hour, or until the tomatoes are slightly brown and shriveled. Remove from the oven and set aside.

BOILED DRESSING

MAKES 1 CUP

John Fleer, a great contemporary Southern chef, was the first person I ever saw cook boiled dressing. I had never heard of such a thing. On first description it ran against my Northern sensibilities. At the time, John was chef at Blackberry Farm, the stunning Relais & Châteaux property in Walland, Tennessee. I remember John did a strawberry soup demo and then another demo on boiled dressing. The boiled dressing stuck in my head, and when that happens it ends up on menus. This dressing is like a sauce for all. It does need to be paired with something rich because this is another high-acid dressing.

¼ cup cider vinegar
2 egg yolks
¼ teaspoon granulated sugar
½ teaspoon dry mustard
1 teaspoon all-purpose flour
Pinch of cayenne
¼ teaspoon kosher salt, plus more to taste
¼ teaspoon freshly ground black pepper
1 teaspoon unsalted butter
¼ cup heavy cream
1 tablespoon crème fraîche
1 tablespoon freshly squeezed lemon juice

Pour the vinegar into a small saucepan over medium-high and bring to a boil.

Put the egg yolks in a small metal bowl and whisk in the sugar, dry mustard, flour, cayenne, salt, and pepper. Create a restaurant-grade double boiler: Find a pot that the metal bowl with egg-yolk mixture can nestle into but not fit all the way into. Add an inch of water to the pot and set over medium heat. Place the small metal bowl with the yolk mixture on top of the pot.

Slowly whisk the boiling vinegar into the egg-yolk mixture. If you feel like it's getting too hot you can always pull the bowl off the pot below. Cook the mixture over the double boiler until it has thickened to a light custard and is just beginning to bubble. If you cook further you will have vinegar-sugar scrambled eggs, so remove from the heat! Add the butter to the custard, whisking all the while, then add the cream and crème fraîche.

Cool, then mix in the lemon juice. Season with salt to taste. The dressing will keep for a week in the fridge.

CAESAR SALAD

2 heads of romaine lettuce, outer leaves removed, cored, washed, and laid out to dry

12 bacon slices, cooked and cut into 1-inch-long pieces

¼ cup grated Parmigiano-Reggiano

1½ cups Croutons (recipe follows)

½ cup Caesar Dressing (recipe follows)

Freshly ground black pepper

My dad, Keith, is not, per se, a gastronome. This is a man who orders Pinot Grigio thinking it's a red. But he does have a great palate and knows good food when he eats it. Like me, his staple diet could consist mostly of citrus fruit, carrots, great bread, and Caesar salad. Dad has made his version of Caesar for decades and it is really good stuff. Mine is similar with the same reliance on garlic, hot sauce, and Worcestershire, but is more refined than the fatherly version.

Tear the lettuce into 2 by 2-inch pieces and place into a medium to large salad bowl. Add the bacon, Parmigiano-Reggiano, croutons, and the Caesar dressing. Toss well to combine. Season evenly with salt. Finish with pepper and serve immediately.

SERVES 6

CAESAR DRESSING

MAKES 2 CUPS

2 garlic cloves, minced
2 salt-packed anchovies, rinsed and minced
1 tablespoon Dijon mustard
1 tablespoon freshly squeezed lemon juice
1 tablespoon sherry vinegar
1 egg yolk
¾ cup olive oil
1 teaspoon Worcestershire sauce
¼ teaspoon hot sauce
¼ teaspoon kosher salt
⅛ teaspoon freshly ground black pepper

In a clean stainless-steel mixing bowl, mix the garlic, anchovies, Dijon, lemon juice, and sherry vinegar. Set aside.

Set another clean stainless-steel mixing bowl over a damp dish towel to keep it from moving around when you are whisking. Add the egg yolk to the bowl and then slowly drizzle in the olive oil, whisking to emulsify and make a mayonnaise base. Keep whisking until all of the oil is incorporated, then add the garlic and anchovy mixture and blend well. Add the Worcestershire, hot sauce, salt, and pepper, and blend well. Pour the dressing into a Mason jar and store in the fridge until ready to use.

CROUTONS

5 cups ½-inch by ½-inch crustless bread cubes
1 cup clarified butter (page 149), warmed
2 tablespoons minced garlic
Salt and freshly ground black pepper

Preheat the oven to 400°F.

Toss the bread with the butter, the garlic, and salt and pepper to taste. Spread the bread cubes in an even layer on a rimmed baking sheet. Toast in the oven until nicely colored but not burnt. These croutons should have just a touch of chewiness in the middle surrounded by a nice crisp exterior.

A Message About Community

My mantra is this: local first, sustainable second, organic third. Local has impact and impact produces change. Change is the process of making the farming sustainable, and once sustainable the next step is certified organically grown. The demand for immediate and complete change by some food advocates is one that just is not feasible for most farmers and one that the average consumer cannot yet afford. Small steps will win this race and those first small steps are about your local sphere. The small steps that you take as a consumer are multifold: Shop at your farmer's market, buy local crafts and art, frequent local independent restaurants, buy locally roasted coffee, buy native plants, learn how to garden, don't eat overly processed foods, know the person who raises your eggs. This has nothing to do with a political stance and everything to do with a community stance. I am not a fanatic, just a believer. I believe in the place we live and in finding ways to make it great every day. I am endlessly enamored of my local sphere, my community.

There are people in this country who are changing the system for all the right reasons and making headway that I had never thought possible. People like Michel Nischan, the New York–based chef who started a group called Wholesome Wave. Michel and his co-conspirators were concerned that local, sustainable, and organic foods were only available to a small sliver of the community and advocated a system where WIC and federal food stamps would be worth twice their face value at local farmer's markets. (WIC is the federal government's Special Supplemental Nutrition Program for Women, Infants, and Children.) Wholesome Wave has directly impacted diet and obesity issues by changing the way people eat. This makes community stronger. This is a game changer.

At the restaurants we strive to create a learning environment at all times. We want to be endowed with endless curiosity about food and wine. As opposed to many service industry spots, we enjoy knowing what we know but never want the baggage of pomp and circumstance to taint that excitement. I preach that as a dental assistant needs to know teeth, the waiters, cooks, bussers, and hosts need to know food and wine. This sounds basic, but it is not the norm in restaurants. It's an endless topic and we treasure the daily learning.

Our restaurants have broad appeal to be available to most of the community. Some of our community members have the ability to eat with us four times weekly. Some treat us as a yearly celebratory spot. Some just come for brunch and some just come for our early evening prix fixe. This ability to serve many levels of society has made us proud. It has made us what we want to be: a great community restaurant.

There are wonderful people in every community and here are two from my community.

* Tim Mills, farmer *   * Alice Mills, farmer *

mule powered

from

SEAS
&

STREAMS

FROGMORE STEW

BRONZED **REDFISH** with LEMON SAUCE, CITRUS & PULLED PARSLEY

GIGGED **FLOUNDER** WITH BOILED-PEANUT BUERRE BLANC

BACON-WRAPPED, FENNEL-STUFFED **TROUT** WITH HOT-PEPPER VINAIGRETTE

SALMON WITH MARINATED VEGETABLES & SALMORIGLIO

SEARED AND POACHED **HALIBUT** WITH SNAP PEAS & SALSA VERDE

GRILLED **MAHI MAHI** WITH HOT SAUCE BUERRE BLANC

SEARED DAY-BOAT **SCALLOPS** WITH COLLARDS, POTLIKKER & CRISP GRIT DISCS

CRISP **CATFISH** WITH TOMATO CHUTNEY & VERMOUTH EMULSION

CORNMEAL-DUSTED **SKATE** WITH CANE BLACK BUTTER

SHRIMP WITH ANDOUILLE AND HOMINY GRITS

SIX COMPOUND BUTTERS

Unless you were a Navy brat, a surfer prodigy, or a very lucky child who lived near a beach, you probably did not eat much fresh fish in your early years. For a nation with as much coastline as we have, our fish gets loved in frozen, processed forms most of the time.

When I was young in Ottawa, a midsize landlocked city, our chances of having fresh red snapper or locally gigged flounder were nil. There were fishmongers in the market and an adequate selection at the supermarkets, but we had average palates and that was not how our family shopped. No chance at all. My memories of fish as a child were of fish sticks, frozen shrimp, and canned smoked oysters. Keith, my much loved father, was a great opener of cans and cooked some good rice to go with the fish sticks, but they were still just haddock with a breadcrumb batter.

There were a couple of exceptions. Until I was eleven, in the middle of summer Duncan Gordon, my mother's godfather and close friend of my late grandfather, would come to our cottage north of Toronto, bringing massive wild salmon from Restigouche, Québec. Restigouche is very remote and he would fly in on a pontoon plane, fish, and then come back to Ontario. Every year those wonderful fish would be poached and cooked in time for my aunt Kathy's birthday. I also remember the lobster houses of New Brunswick and Nova Scotia on a summer road trip and the clam digging we did there. But that was about it. Fish had as important a role in my childhood as grade-seven Latin— which is to say, a few lasting moments that stick with you, but not many.

So much of my knowledge about fish and shellfish has come from just being in the restaurant, ordering what we want and figuring out where it comes from. The beauty showed through when I realized the local abundance off our coast.

We have learned about the seafood seasons and how to plan with them. Spring is halibut and beans, summer is shrimp and tomatoes, fall is scallops and escarole, and winter is bass and shallots. I begin my week looking forward to what new fish will be available. We change the menus at the restaurants so often that we are able to grasp the seasons with a big culinary hug.

EAST COAST SHRIMP

Fresh Tomato Juice but I also love Sacramento brand...

unsalted butter

LEEKS

ANDOUILLE

GARLIC

new Potatoes

REAL TOMATOES !

celery

white corn but yellow is good too!

fresh thyme

OLD BAY

lemons give brightness

FROGMORE STEW

My take on this classic Southern seafood boil was partly inspired by a recipe in Hoppin' John Taylor's first book, *Hoppin' John's Lowcountry Cooking.* Rather than using the cooking liquid just as a cooking medium, I make it into a brothy meal, much like a bouillabaisse or cioppino. Make it as spicy as you want with the addition of some nice smoky chiles, such as chipotles.

Old Bay seasoning is one of the few shortcuts we ever take in the restaurant, but it's tried and true.

⬤ ⬤

2 tablespoons extra-virgin olive oil

1 leek, white part only, cleaned (see Note page 242) and thinly sliced (½ cup)

1 cup chopped fresh tomatoes

¼ cup finely diced celery

1 garlic clove, minced

½ tablespoon chopped fresh thyme leaves

1 cup dry white wine

1 cup tomato juice

3 cups fish stock (or clam juice in a pinch)

9 new potatoes, golf-ball size

3 ears of corn, shucked and cut into quarters

1 pound andouille sausage

1 teaspoon Old Bay seasoning

1½ teaspoons kosher salt

1½ pounds fresh large shrimp, heads off, peeled but with the very end of the tail shell intact

1 cup arugula, lightly chopped

2 tablespoons unsalted butter

1 tablespoon chopped fresh flat-leaf parsley

3 lemon rounds, ⅛ inch thick, seeds removed

6 thick slices of grilled country bread, for serving

Place a medium to large pot with a lid over medium heat. Once hot, add the olive oil, then the leeks. Sauté until just translucent, about 3 minutes, and add the tomatoes, celery, garlic, and thyme. Sauté for 3 more minutes and add the white wine; reduce by half. Then add the tomato juice, fish stock, potatoes, corn, and sausage. Cook for 5 minutes and add the Old Bay and ½ teaspoon of the salt.

Season the shrimp with ½ teaspoon of the salt. Add the shrimp to the pot, cover with a lid, and cook for 5 minutes, until the shrimp are cooked through and turn shiny white.

Add the arugula and butter. Stir into the shrimp stew. Add the parsley and lemon and season with the remaining ½ teaspoon of salt.

Ladle the stew into 6 bowls and garnish with a slice of grilled bread for sopping up the broth.

SERVES 6

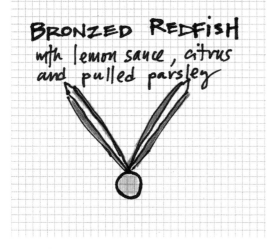

BRONZED REDFISH
with lemon sauce, citrus and pulled parsley

1 cup white wine

1 branch of fresh thyme

2 shallots, minced

1 teaspoon grated lemon zest

1 tablespoon freshly squeezed lemon juice

1 cup clam juice

1 teaspoon heavy cream

¼ pound (1 stick) cold unsalted butter, cut into ½-inch cubes

½ teaspoon smoked sweet paprika

½ teaspoon finely chopped fresh thyme

¼ teaspoon cayenne

1 teaspoon dried oregano

½ teaspoon ground cumin seeds, lightly toasted

¼ teaspoon toasted and ground allspice seeds

¼ teaspoon freshly ground black pepper

1 teaspoon canola oil

4 (6-ounce) redfish fillets

¼ teaspoon kosher salt

1 navel orange, cut into supremes (see photo, page 81)

½ cup fresh flat-leaf parsley leaves

1 teaspoon Shallot-Thyme Vinaigrette (page 111)

This is my version of the Paul Prudhomme classic.

Wild saltwater redfish is a rarity these days. Luckily there are some really great farms raising clean, sustainable, and healthy redfish.

My rendition of Prudhomme's recipe uses a bronzing method of cooking rather than blackening and goes a little lighter on the spice to showcase the beauty of the fish. It is also accompanied by a simple and healthier version of a beurre blanc, with an increased acid punch of lemon. Serve with Duck Liver Dirty Rice (page 235).

Preheat the oven to 400°F.

In a medium pot, combine the wine, thyme, shallots, lemon zest, and lemon juice and place over medium heat. Cook to reduce the volume by half and add the clam juice. Reduce by two-thirds to yield ½ cup of liquid. Add the cream and reduce the heat to low. Slowly whisk in the butter to mount the sauce. Once all the butter has been whisked in, remove the pot from the heat and hold in a warm water bath until ready to use.

To make the bronzing seasoning, combine the paprika, thyme, cayenne, oregano, cumin, allspice, and black pepper in a Mason jar. Cover the jar and shake to combine.

Heat the oil in a large cast-iron pan until it's hot. While the oil is heating, season the fish with salt and sprinkle 1 teaspoon of the seasoning on each portion.

Cook the fish skin side down for 5 minutes, then turn and cook for 4 minutes on the other side. Place the pan in the oven for 2 minutes, then remove the pan and let it rest for 1 minute before serving. The rule is 10 minutes of cooking time for every inch of flesh.

Place the fillets on a platter and liberally sauce them with the lemon sauce. In a small bowl combine the oranges, parsley, and vinaigrette. Toss well and scatter over the fish.

SERVES 4

NOTE: To toast cumin seeds, add to a sauté pan and toast for 30 seconds to 1 minute over low heat.

The flounder season along the southern Atlantic coast picks up in mid- to late summer and lasts through the fall. East Coast–gigged flounder is what I look for. Gigging is the spear fishing for shallow-water coastal fish using a two- or three-pronged trident. It is a primitive method but fishing like Poseidon is pretty cool! In this recipe, the boiled peanuts plump up the buerre blanc. Serve the flounder with buttered Hominy Grits (page 233).

GIGGED FLOUNDER with boiled-peanut buerre blanc

● ●

Preheat the oven to 450°F.

Place a medium saucepan over medium-high heat. Add the shallots, vinegar, wine, bouquet garni, and peppercorns. Reduce by half. Remove the bouquet garni and reduce the heat to low. Pour the reduction through a fine strainer and discard the solids. Return the liquid to the saucepan and cook over low heat. Once the reduction is warm again, slowly add the ¼ pound of butter 1 cube at a time, whisking continuously until all of the butter has been incorporated. Finish the sauce with the lemon zest, orange zest, garlic, and boiled peanuts. Season with the pinch of salt and hold in a warm spot off the heat until ready to use.

Bring a large fry pan to medium-high heat on the stovetop. Season the fish on both sides with the ¼ teaspoon of salt and add the oil to the pan. When the oil is hot and shimmery add the fish and cook, untouched, for 3 minutes. When the fish begins to pull back from the pan, turn it over and cook for 1 minute on the other side. Add the remaining tablespoon of butter to the pan and place in the oven for 5 minutes, or until the fish is fully cooked, no longer gelatinous in the center, solid white in flake, and no longer translucent.

Arrange the fish portions on 4 plates and finish with a tablespoon of sauce on each.

SERVES 4

2 shallots, minced

1 cup champagne vinegar

1 cup white wine

Small bouquet garni of fresh thyme and tarragon (see drawing, page 99)

3 black peppercorns

¼ pound plus 1 tablespoon cold unsalted butter, cut into ½ by ½-inch cubes

¼ teaspoon grated lemon zest

¼ teaspoon grated orange zest

½ teaspoon minced garlic

½ cup shelled Boiled Peanuts (page 56)

¼ teaspoon plus a pinch of kosher salt

4 (5-ounce) flounder fillets

1 tablespoon vegetable oil

bacon-wrapped fennel-stuffed TROUT with hot-pepper vinaigrette

Trout farming has come a long way and trout is now considered by Seafood Watch to be among the best choices in sustainable seafood consumption. Many of the great trout farms are within a two-hour drive from us here in northeast Georgia.

When wrapping trout in bacon, use thinly sliced bacon. For something like this I use Nueske bacon from Wisconsin and ask the butcher to slice it razor thin.

Hot pepper vinegar is a staple of most meat-and-three restaurants in the South. You can easily make your own (see page 265) or Texas Pete has a nice bottled version. Serve with braised cabbage (see page 218), Cornmeal Campfire Tomatoes (page 227), and simply dressed frisée.

1 tablespoon unsalted butter

½ fennel bulb, cored, cut into ⅛-inch-thick wedges

1 leek, cleaned (see Note page 242) and sliced into ⅛-inch-thick rounds

1 teaspoon chopped fresh thyme

¼ cup Chicken Stock (page 179)

2 (8-ounce) trout, headless and butterflied

1 teaspoon kosher salt

6 strips of thinly sliced applewood smoked bacon (approximately 1 ounce per strip)

2 tablespoons clarified butter (page 149)

1 teaspoon finely minced shallot

2 tablespoons hot pepper vinegar

¼ cup extra-virgin olive oil

¼ teaspoon smoked paprika

¼ teaspoon freshly cracked black pepper

Preheat the oven to 400°F.

In a 10-inch sauté pan over medium heat, add the butter. As it's gently melting, add the fennel, leek, and thyme. Cook gently for 2 minutes. Add the chicken stock and bring to a gentle simmer for 3 minutes or until the fennel and leek are tender throughout. Remove from the pan onto a large plate and allow to cool.

Lay the trout skin side down on a large cutting board and season with ½ teaspoon of the salt. Place half of the fennel and leek mixture on each of the lower fillets and then fold the other hinged fillet on top, creating a sandwich.

Overlap three strips of bacon on a clean plate. Place one of the stuffed trout over the bacon. Roll the bacon around the trout. Repeat this for the second trout.

Place a 12-inch cast-iron pan over medium-high heat and add the clarified butter. When the butter foams and sputters add the wrapped trout to the pan and let them cook for 2 minutes. Turn the fish, cook for 2 minutes more, and then transfer to the oven. Continue cooking for 6 minutes.

To make the hot pepper vinaigrette, whisk together the minced shallot, hot pepper vinegar, olive oil, smoked paprika, black pepper, and remaining ½ teaspoon of salt.

Once the fish comes out of the oven, slice each trout in half, yielding a front half and a tail half. Present the halved wrapped fish on individual plates with a healthy tablespoon of the hot pepper vinaigrette on each portion.

SERVES 4

CLARIFIED BUTTER

Butter is an emulsification of butterfat, milk solids, and water. Clarifying means separating the three, discarding the milk solids, cooking away the water, and keeping the fat, or ghee. The cleaned-up butterfat will withstand much higher cooking temperatures than regular butter before smoking, yet still gives us a richly flavored cooking oil.

1 pound unsalted butter

In a medium saucepan over low heat, melt the butter. Skim the milk solids that rise to the top. Continue to discard the solids until the melted butter becomes yellow and clear. The clarified butter will keep in the fridge for 1 week.

This is a very colorful, beautiful, and healthy dish that shows off so many of the things that I love about spring: salmon and vegetables. My kids love salmon so we eat a lot of this dish come salmon season. I usually wait for the season to be open for a while before I buy. Late April or May is a good time. Those early prices are often pressured by excitement and the price usually comes down after a couple of weeks. There is nothing better than a true Copper River King salmon from Alaska.

I listed a vast array of vegetables in the dish but you could hunt down what's best in your market and use the same technique. The salmoriglio sauce is a simple Southern Italian sauce usually paired with grilled meats, but it works so well with this salmon. The lemon and herbs just have an affinity with the salmon that is so natural.

I like to cook salmon until it is a little less than medium, with a thin red-orange streak of rare going through the center.

* *

Preheat the oven to 400°F.

Cut the green beans into 1-inch lengths and place in a large bowl. Add the tomatoes, squash, celery, carrots, and scallions. Add the vinaigrette and gently toss. Season with ¼ teaspoon of the salt and add the mint, thyme, and parsley. Set aside at room temperature while you roast the salmon.

In a large oven-safe fry pan warm the olive oil over medium-high heat. Evenly season the salmon fillets with the ¾ teaspoon of remaining salt.

When the oil is just about smoking, place the salmon in the pan. The key to cooking this is knowing that the timer starts as soon as the salmon hits the pan. The total cooking time should be 10 minutes per every inch of thickness at the thickest part of the fish. Let the salmon cook for 3 minutes, then turn it over. Cook for 3 minutes more, turn again, and place in the oven for 4 minutes.

Remove the pan from the oven and place the salmon fillets on a platter. Put 4 plates on the counter and place a salmon fillet on each one. Liberally sauce with salmoriglio and a heap of the marinated vegetables.

Eat immediately.

SERVES 4

SALMON
with
marinated vegetables
and salmoriglio

16 green beans, blanched until tender

8 cherry tomatoes, halved

6 small pattypan squash, cut thin

2 celery stalks, peeled and diced

2 carrots, julienned

2 scallions, cut on the diagonal

¼ cup Shallot-Thyme Vinaigrette (page 111)

1 teaspoon sea salt

1 teaspoon fresh mint leaves

1 teaspoon chopped fresh thyme

1 tablespoon chopped fresh flat-leaf parsley

1 tablespoon olive oil

4 (5- to 6-ounce) wild salmon fillets, about 1 inch thick, skin removed

¾ cup Salmoriglio (recipe follows)

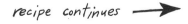
recipe continues ⟶

SALMORIGLIO

MAKES ¾ CUP

This is a versatile sauce that works well with grilled meats and roasted fish or shellfish. It is also great drizzled on tomatoes in the summertime.

3 tablespoons freshly squeezed lemon juice
4 tablespoons extra-virgin olive oil
1 tablespoon chopped fresh marjoram (or oregano)
¼ teaspoon red pepper flakes

1 teaspoon rinsed and chopped anchovies
½ teaspoon grated lemon zest
3 garlic cloves, minced
¼ teaspoon fine sea salt
¼ teaspoon freshly ground black pepper

In a small bowl, combine the lemon juice and olive oil. Add the marjoram, red pepper flakes, anchovies, lemon zest, garlic, sea salt, and black pepper. The sauce will keep for a week in the fridge.

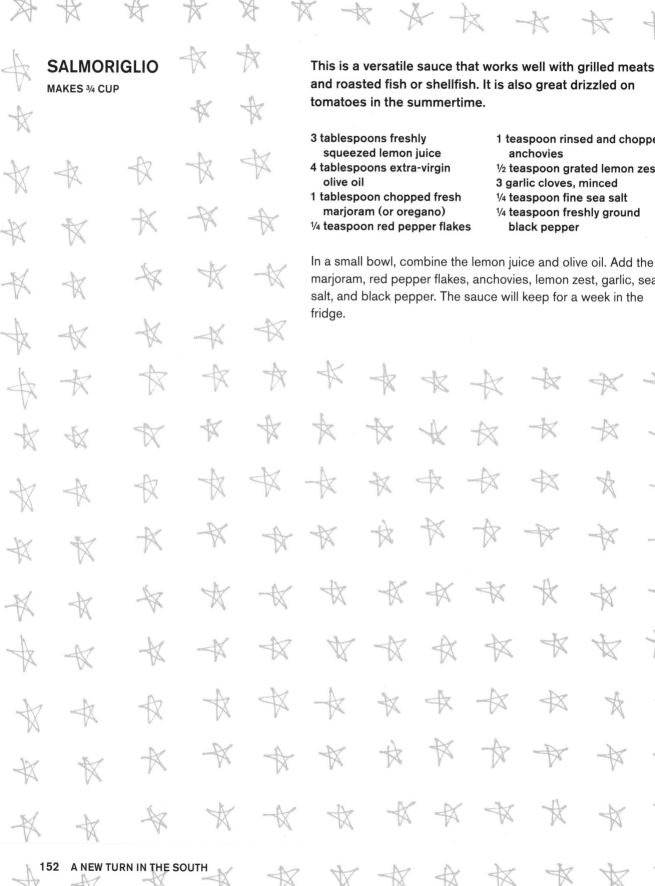

WHY THINGS STICK TO PANS...

I am no scientist, but I have a theory. The metal that our pots are made of, such as stainless steel, cast iron, or enameled cast iron, is slighted pitted or porous at room temperature but gets smooth when hot. If you put protein in a room-temperature pan and then heat it up, the protein droops into those little pits and then the pan expands around the protein, basically grabbing it and causing protein stickage. But if you let the pan heat up enough, the chances of the protein sticking are greatly diminished. Try it. It would be a good science-fair project.

This method of searing, introducing a broth, and finishing in the oven or on the stovetop is a great method that usually requires only one pan. Halibut shines in this preparation but cod, bass, swordfish, or snapper would work too; just remember to remove the skin. A straight-sided fry pan with a lid is perfect for this recipe.

• •

Preheat the oven to 375°F.

Place a 4-quart pot of water on the stove and bring to a boil for the snap peas.

Place the halibut fillets onto a large plate and season on all sides with ½ teaspoon of the kosher salt. Heat a 12-inch fry pan with a lid over high heat and add the clarified butter. When the butter is hot and shimmering carefully add the fish to the pan. Let the fish cook for 3 minutes, untouched, then turn the fish over carefully and reduce the heat to a simmer. Add the shallot, the vermouth, chicken stock, bay leaf, and thyme. Cover and place in the oven for 3 to 5 minutes, depending on the thickness of the fish. When done, the halibut will be entirely opaque and, when a tiny incision is made, the fish will be very soft.

Remove the halibut from the pan and place on a warm platter. Strain the hot braising liquid into a saucepan and whisk in the cold butter. Set the sauce aside in a warm spot until the snap peas are ready.

Cook the peas in the boiling water for 1 minute and then remove to a bowl using a slotted spoon. Add the crème fraîche, lemon zest, and parsley to the peas. Toss well to coat and season with the remaining ½ teaspoon of salt. Discard the bay leaf. Pour the sauce over the halibut fillets. Top each piece of fish with a tablespoon of salsa verde and an arrangement of warm peas.

SERVES 4

seared
+
poached
HALIBUT
with
snap peas
&
salsa verde

4 (5-ounce) thick halibut fillets

¾ teaspoon kosher salt

2 tablespoons clarified butter (page 149)

1 finely minced shallot

¼ cup dry vermouth

½ cup Chicken Stock (see page 179)

1 bay leaf

5 sprigs of fresh thyme

1 tablespoon cold unsalted butter

8 ounces sugar snap peas, strings removed, cut in half lengthwise

2 tablespoons crème fraîche

¼ teaspoon grated lemon zest

1 teaspoon chopped fresh flat-leaf parsley

1 teaspoon chopped fresh thyme leaves

4 tablespoons Salsa Verde (recipe follows)

recipe continues →

SALSA VERDE

MAKES ABOUT 2 CUPS

I love fresh herbs, and they are easy to grow in Georgia. Mint, marjoram, and parsley grow like weeds here. Basil isn't as easy because we regularly oscillate between drought and flood. Growing herbs on the back porch in pots makes life much more predictable.

Salsa verde will keep in the fridge for about three days and longer if you cover it with a little extra-virgin olive oil to seal it from the air. You could freeze it in ice trays as well, just like you did back in the 1980s with all that basil pesto.

½ cup fresh flat-leaf parsley, leaves only, finely chopped
1 tablespoon fresh basil, leaves only, finely chopped
1 tablespoon fresh mint, leaves only, finely chopped
1 tablespoon fresh marjoram, leaves only, finely chopped
¾ cup extra-virgin olive oil, plus more to taste
2 garlic cloves, peeled and minced

Pinch of red pepper flakes
1 tablespoon salt-packed capers, rinsed well and chopped
1 tablespoon rinsed and minced anchovy fillets
1 teaspoon Dijon mustard
1 tablespoon red wine vinegar
Kosher salt and freshly ground black pepper

Place the parsley, basil, mint, and marjoram in a bowl and pour in the olive oil. Add the garlic, red pepper flakes, capers, and chopped anchovies. Stir well. Add the mustard and the vinegar. Season and thin if necessary with more olive oil. Season with salt and pepper but remember that capers and anchovies are already inherently salty. Salsa verde will last for 4 days in the fridge.

GRILLED MAHI MAHI WITH HOT SAUCE BUERRE BLANC

Mahimahi is one of the best fish for grilling. It is one of the few sustainable wild fish choices we still have. It grows quickly and is abundant along our coasts.

This recipe pairs the fish with an assertive sauce and then cools it back down with some very simply prepared cucumbers. It is great summer eating that begs for a nice local beer.

The amount of hot sauce in the recipe seems like a lot, but the buttery sauce tempers it. Make sure you use a Louisiana-style hot sauce like Texas Pete and not Tabasco, which is too spicy for this dish.

1 English cucumber, thinly sliced

¾ teaspoon Maldon sea salt

2 tablespoons olive oil

2 tablespoons freshly squeezed lemon juice

1 tablespoon minced fresh flat-leaf parsley

1 shallot, minced

½ cup cider vinegar

2 tablespoons hot sauce (Louisiana-style, such as Texas Pete)

¼ pound (1 stick) cold unsalted butter, cubed

4 (6-ounce) mahimahi fillets

4 lemon wedges

Place the cucumber slices in a 2-quart mixing bowl and season with ¼ teaspoon of the sea salt. Drizzle the cucumbers with 1 tablespoon of the olive oil and 1 tablespoon of the lemon juice, add the parsley, and toss to combine. Let sit at room temperature as you complete the other steps.

Get a grill going. If you are cooking on charcoal get it lit about 45 minutes before you grill to let the briquets get gray and cooked down. Meanwhile, start the sauce.

In a 1-quart saucepan, combine the shallot, cider vinegar, and the remaining tablespoon of lemon juice. Place over medium heat and reduce to almost 2 tablespoons of liquid. Add the hot sauce, reduce the heat to a bare simmer, and begin slowly whisking in the cold butter. Season with a pinch of salt and keep warm in a water bath.

Place the mahimahi portions on a plate and season with the remaining sea salt. Drizzle the last tablespoon of olive oil over the fish. Grill over high heat for 3 minutes, then flip and cook for 3 minutes longer, or until fully cooked with nice grill marks.

Arrange the cucumbers on a platter and place the grilled mahimahi on top. Drizzle with beurre blanc and serve with a wedge of lemon.

SERVES 4

"Day-boat" refers to a boat that goes out for a day and brings back the catch the same day, versus massive trawlers that go out for weeks on end. "U10" means there are fewer than ten shucked scallops per pound, so U10 scallops are pretty big.

There are many keys to searing scallops and fish in general. The seafood needs to be dry and should go into a hot stainless-steel pan. Don't crowd the pan, as that encourages steaming. You need to have lots of patience before turning the scallops. Having a good hood vent helps.

seared day-boat SCALLOPS with Collards, potlikker and crisp grit discs

½ cup yellow grits
¾ teaspoon kosher salt
2½ tablespoons cold unsalted butter
12 sea scallops (U10)
½ teaspoon chopped fresh thyme
2 tablespoons clarified butter (page 149)
1 cup Collard Greens (page 222), finely chopped
½ cup potlikker from Collard Greens (see page 222)

Preheat the oven to 375°F.

Bring 2 cups water to a boil. Whisk in the yellow grits and reduce the heat to low, stirring regularly for 55 minutes. Once the grits are cooked add ¼ teaspoon of the salt and ½ tablespoon of the cold butter, and stir well with a whisk. Using 1 additional tablespoon of the cold butter, coat the bottom of a 9½-inch pie pan. Pour the grits into the pie pan and spread evenly, then cool the grits in the refrigerator for 45 minutes. Once cool, cut the grits, using a 3-inch round cookie cutter, into 4 round discs and set aside.

Heat a 12-inch stainless-steel fry pan over medium heat. On a large plate, lay out the scallops and season with the remaining ½ teaspoon of kosher salt and the thyme. Add 1 tablespoon of the clarified butter into the hot pan. Make sure the butter is hot before adding the scallops one at a time. Cook the scallops for 3 minutes, then turn them over and cook for another 3 minutes. Place the fry pan in the oven for 2 minutes.

While the scallops are in the oven, heat a large (at least 10-inch) nonstick pan over medium-high heat. When the pan is hot, add the remaining tablespoon of clarified butter. When the butter is hot, add the grit cakes. Crisp for 3 minutes, turn, and place the pan in the oven for 3 minutes.

Heat the collards over low heat in a small saucepan with ½ tablespoon of the cold butter. Heat the potlikker in a small saucepan and whisk in the remaining ½ tablespoon of cold butter. On individual plates, place a crisp grit cake off center. Put ¼ cup collards in the center of the plate with 3 scallops arranged on top. Drizzle the potlikker jus over the scallops and serve.

SERVES 4

Talk about having a rough time in life if you're a "bottom feeder." Catfish deserves better billing. It is one of the few truly sustainable fish in North America with sound farming practices. Imported catfish is usually from China, where some farms have toxic waters. China raises about three quarters of our imported fish so it's hard to avoid, but you should try to buy domestic.

In this recipe the little whiskered guys come out of the oven with a nice crisp crust and tender flesh. The vermouth sauce mellows the spicy chutney.

The chutney is adapted from a recipe in the book *Flatbreads and Flavors,* by Jeffrey Alford and Naomi Duguid, two prominent cookbook authors from Toronto. The seductive flavor that dominates is the fenugreek, but be careful not to use too much.

Note on the recipe name: before I called this sauce an emulsion, I just called it a vermouth sauce. One day I printed all the menus without the "VER." Catfish with Mouth Sauce. That did not sell well.

This goes well with simply dressed arugula and Yellow Grits (page 234).

CRISP CATFISH with tomato chutney & vermouth emulsion

4 (6-ounce) fresh catfish fillets, trimmed of any connective tissue

¼ teaspoon kosher salt

⅛ teaspoon freshly ground black pepper

1 cup panko (Japanese bread crumbs)

1 tablespoon chile powder

2 tablespoons vegetable oil

4 tablespoons Vermouth Emulsion (recipe follows)

4 tablespoons Tomato Chutney (page 264)

Preheat the oven to 400°F.

Season the fillets with the salt and pepper and set aside.

Place the panko on a wide plate or bowl and add the chile powder. Mix lightly to incorporate the chile powder. Gently press each fillet into the panko on both sides. Set aside.

Warm a large fry pan on high heat and add the oil. When the oil is shimmering, place the catfish fillets in the pan and cook for 3 minutes on each side. Finish in the oven for 4 more minutes. Remove the catfish from the pan and set aside as you plate.

Pool a tablespoon of vermouth emulsion on each plate and place a fish fillet on that pool. Spoon a tablespoon of chutney on each fillet and nap a bit more vermouth emulsion over each one.

SERVES 4

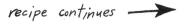

recipe continues ⟶

VERMOUTH EMULSION

1 cup dry vermouth
1 sprig of fresh thyme
1 shallot, minced
¼ cup clam juice
1 teaspoon freshly squeezed
  lemon juice

1 tablespoon heavy cream
¼ pound (1 stick) unsalted
  butter, cold and cut into
  ½-inch cubes
Pinch of sea salt

Combine the vermouth with the thyme, shallot, clam juice, and lemon juice in a small saucepan and place over medium-high heat. Bring to a boil, then reduce to low, and reduce by two-thirds. You should have about ⅓ cup of liquid. Strain and discard the solids. Place the liquid back in the pan over low heat. Add the cream and slowly whisk the butter into the reduction. Pull the pan away from the heat if it gets too hot, to prevent breaking. Season with salt and hold in a water bath until the catfish is ready.

In the South, skate is commonly considered a bait fish. But up north and in Europe, skate is a prized dinner fish. It also makes a good crisp fish sandwich.

Skate is a ray (or *raie* in French) with a tender flesh. It cooks quickly on or off the bone and has a very clear way of telling you not to eat it: Once it's past its prime, skate smells like ammonia.

The black butter in this recipe is just a brown butter with vinegar. The process is similar to clarifying butter (see page 000) but higher heat is used so the milk solids actually brown. If you burn the milk solids, you'll need to start over.

I would serve this with Shiitake Slaw (page 209), Brussels sprout leaves, or steamed spinach.

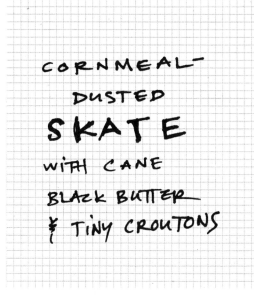

CORNMEAL-DUSTED SKATE WITH CANE BLACK BUTTER & TINY CROUTONS

● ●

Preheat the oven to 400°F.

To make the croutons, melt ¼ cup (4 tablespoons) of the butter in a small saucepan and combine with the diced bread in a large bowl. Toss well, place on a rimmed baking sheet, and bake until nicely toasted, about 5 minutes. Remove from the oven and reduce the heat to 200°F.

Place the skate on a large plate and season both sides with ¼ teaspoon of the salt. Pour the cornmeal into a large baking dish and dredge the fish in the cornmeal on both sides.

Warm the clarified butter in a large cast-iron pan over medium-high heat. Place 2 portions of the skate into the pan and cook until they are nicely browned and crisp, about 3 minutes on each side. Transfer the skate to a cooling rack perched over a baking sheet and hold in the warm oven. Repeat the steps with the remaining skate.

When the last of the skate goes into the oven, it is time to make the black butter. Place a 2-quart pan on the stove over medium heat. Add the remaining ¼ cup butter and melt. Cook until the butter froths and then the milk solids separate and start to brown. When everything looks nicely toasted, turn off the heat and add the vinegar, parsley, and remaining ¼ teaspoon of salt.

Place the skate on a platter and garnish with the croutons. Stir the warm black butter well and spoon over the skate.

½ cup (1 stick) unsalted butter

1 cup diced sourdough bread (¼-inch dice; crust on is fine)

4 (6-ounce) pieces of boneless skate

½ teaspoon kosher salt

2 cups fine white cornmeal

2 tablespoons clarified butter (page 149)

2 tablespoons cane vinegar (see page 67)

1 tablespoon minced fresh flat-leaf parsley

SKATE. *raja erinacea.*

SERVES 4

SHRIMP with andouille & hominy grits

We get our hominy grits from Anson Mills in Columbia, South Carolina, but there are a number of great grist mills dotting the South for you to choose from.

Hominy is made of corn kernels that have been nixtamalized, dried, and then ground. Nixtamalization is the process of soaking in an alkaline solution, which plumps up the corn and makes the corn more digestible through the conversion of niacin. The same alkaline, or lime solution, is often used to crisp cucumbers prior to pickling.

This shrimp and grits recipe is the work of Dean Neff, favorite sous. Favorite sous is the restaurant equivalent of favorite son. Dean is from Tybee Island, Georgia, and they sure know their seafood down that way.

I love shrimp and grits for breakfast, lunch, or dinner.

* * *

¾ teaspoon kosher salt

¾ cup hominy grits

4 tablespoons (½ stick) cold unsalted butter

½ cup minced sweet onion

2 celery stalks, minced (¼ cup)

½ pound andouille sausage chopped into ¼-inch cubes

1 garlic clove, thinly sliced

½ cup chopped roasted red peppers

2 plum tomatoes, peeled, seeded, and diced

1 teaspoon Old Bay seasoning

¼ teaspoon red pepper flakes

½ cup tomato juice

½ cup clam juice

1 pound (21 to 25 count) peeled and deveined shrimp

1 teaspoon chopped fresh thyme

1 teaspoon chopped fresh flat-leaf parsley

1 tablespoon freshly squeezed lemon juice

In a nonreactive 2-quart saucepan, combine 3 cups water, ½ teaspoon of the salt, and the grits. Place on high heat and bring to a boil, stirring with a whisk. As soon as the water boils, reduce to a simmer. Switch to a wooden spoon as the grits thicken. Cook the grits, stirring every 5 minutes or so, for an hour. Then stir in 2 tablespoons of the butter and set the cooked grits aside.

Melt 1 tablespoon of the butter in a 12-inch fry pan over medium heat, and when the butter bubbles and froths add the onion, celery, and andouille. Cook for 5 minutes, stirring every minute. Add the garlic, red peppers, tomatoes, Old Bay, and red pepper flakes. Cook for 5 more minutes, then add the tomato juice and clam juice. Stir well and reduce the liquid for about 2 minutes.

Season the shrimp with the remaining ¼ teaspoon of salt and add the shrimp to the pan. Stir well to combine and cook them for 5 minutes. The cooked shrimp should be just white, no longer translucent, but not chalky and dry.

Add the remaining tablespoon of butter to the pan and finish with the thyme, parsley, and lemon juice.

Place about ¾ cup of grits on each plate and then spoon a quarter of the stewed shrimp, peppers, and tomatoes over each pile of grits. Serve immediately.

SERVES 4

SIX COMPOUND BUTTERS
1 · 2 · 3 · 4 · 5 · 6

I love the simplicity and versatility of compound butters. They freeze well, too!

This is the method for all of the following. Soften the butter for 1 hour at room temperature. Add the ingredients and blend well. Pack into a small Mason jar or roll into a log using parchment paper, as if you were rolling a butter cigar. Place in the fridge and let chill and set before using. The butters are great to have for adorning roasted fish, a perfect steak, some steamed broccoli, or a simple sandwich.

RADISH BUTTER

- ½ pound (2 sticks) unsalted butter
- ¼ cup fresh radishes cut into matchsticks
- ½ teaspoon Maldon sea salt

ROASTED SHALLOT BUTTER

- ½ pound (2 sticks) unsalted butter
- ¼ cup finely chopped roasted shallots
- ½ teaspoon Maldon sea salt

PIQUILLO & AMONTILLADO SHERRY BUTTER

- ½ pound (2 sticks) unsalted butter
- ¼ cup finely chopped piquillo peppers
- 2 tablespoons Amontillado sherry
- 1 teaspoon chopped fresh flat-leaf parsley

BEURRE MONTPELLIER

- ½ pound unsalted butter
- 1 shallot, minced
- 1 cup watercress, blanched until limp, drained, and finely chopped
- 1 tablespoon minced dill pickle
- 1 teaspoon chopped fresh flat-leaf parsley
- ½ teaspoon minced fresh tarragon
- 2 hard-boiled egg yolks
- 1 tablespoon chopped drained capers
- 1 teaspoon rinsed and minced anchovies

BASIL BUTTER

- ½ pound (2 sticks) unsalted butter
- ½ cup loosely packed basil leaves, blanched for 10 seconds and then shocked in ice water
- ½ teaspoon Maldon sea salt

MISO & LIME BUTTER

- ½ pound (2 sticks) unsalted butter
- ½ teaspoon grated lime zest
- 1 teaspoon freshly squeezed lime juice
- 2 tablespoons blonde miso paste

THINGS
WITH
WINGS

Fried **CHICKEN** with stewed pickled green tomatoes

Grilled **POUSSIN** with lemon, mint and soy

Cane Vinegar Chicken with
pearl onions, orange & spinach

CHICKEN BOG   **BRUNSWICK STEW**

Braised **QUAIL** with leeks, dates, and cider

Fried **QUAIL** breasts with celery root skordalia,
and pomegranate salad

DUCK Choucroute Garnie

Pan-roasted **DUCK** breasts with blueberries,
frisée, caramelized Vidalias & sorghum vinaigrette

Mary and I got excited about the idea of eggs in a hutch. We got excited about the idea of the kids naming the birds and the prospect of calm meanderings of a Mr. Polka foraging the yard for bugs and seeds. We have the requisite henhouse and caged chicken run. Built by our friend Bain, it matched our house, using leftover tin from the roofing job finished years earlier. It was one beautiful chicken coop.

Then the incident occurred. Some neighbors had a rooster who was doing what roosters do well, making lots of noise. Late one evening the rooster got killed by a spiteful neighbor annoyed by the sunrise noise. This prompted a look at the laws for our county and it was found that having chickens within the city limits was completely unlawful . . . as was the cultivation of tomatoes, beans, or other crops for consumption. Basically there was some blanket of laws that prohibit pretty much anything you could possibly eat, whether it made a morning racket or not. The laws are changing slowly to reflect a more progressive agriculture society that we are trying to celebrate, but still, no chickens are allowed in town.

Fowl, the winged world of food, spans many wonderful varieties. Many of them, such as squab, turkey, and goose, were left out of the book for lack of space, rather than by oversight. I love them all, but chicken, poussin, duck, and quail are our larder staples.

FRIED CHICKEN with stewed pickled green tomatoes

4 chicken thighs, approximately
  5 ounces each

1 cup buttermilk

Vegetable shortening

1 teaspoon kosher salt

Pinch of cayenne

Pinch of dry mustard

1 cup all-purpose flour

1 tablespoon unsalted butter

1 tablespoon minced shallot

1 cup chopped ripe red heirloom
  tomatoes

1 cup chopped Pickled Green
  Tomatoes (page 251)

¼ teaspoon chopped serrano chile

1 tablespoon chopped fresh mint

1 tablespoon chopped fresh flat-leaf
  parsley

1 tablespoon Chicken Stock
  (page 179)

I love fried chicken. When we redesigned our home kitchen I installed a pretty major hood to make fried-chicken night a less smoky experience. This means we eat it more often but the smoke detector only goes off once in a while.

My kids love drumsticks and thighs, so that's generally what we cook when it comes to fried chicken. Breasts are just too lean for a satisfying fried dish. The rest of this plate has a great little stew of pickled green tomatoes and fresh red tomatoes, brightened by some chile and mint. It was a recipe written to match up with a Riesling dinner we had at the property of Rebecca Wood, a lauded local potter. That dinner was great and changed me from being a Champagne and fried chicken lover into a Riesling and fried chicken lover. You can still be a canned Pabst chicken lover if you wish.

Place the chicken and buttermilk in a sealable plastic bag and seal tightly. Let it sit in the fridge for 2 to 24 hours.

Place a large cast-iron skillet on medium-high heat and add shortening to a depth of 1 inch. Bring the shortening to 325°F and hold it at that temperature.

Combine the salt, cayenne, and dry mustard in a small bowl and mix well with a fork. Remove the chicken from the bag and place it in a colander over the sink. Discard the bag with buttermilk. Place the chicken on a rimmed baking sheet and dust evenly with the salt mixture.

Place the flour in a large paper bag and then add the chicken. Fold over the top of the bag and shake well to coat the chicken with the flour. Remove the chicken from the bag, shake off the excess flour, and set on a clean baking sheet.

For the stewed pickled tomatoes, melt the butter in a medium-size stainless-steel fry pan over medium-high heat. Add the shallot and cook for 2 minutes, stirring occasionally. Add the red tomatoes and green tomatoes and cook for 7 minutes. Add the serrano chile, mint, parsley, and stock and cook for another 3 minutes. Remove from heat.

Carefully place the chicken, skin side down, into the hot shortening. Cook for 10 minutes and then turn over and cook for another 10 minutes, holding the temperature at 325°F as consistently as possible. Remove the chicken from the pan and place on a cooling rack to drain any excess oil.

Place ½ cup of the tomatoes on each plate and then place a chicken thigh on each pile. Eat.

SERVES 4

A poussin is a young chicken, slaughtered before it reaches twenty-eight days in age. They weigh around a pound each and make a wonderful meal for one person. This recipe is a variation on the classic chicken under a brick. It's finished with a simple herb sauce that takes the blend of soy, lemon, and mustard and matches it with fresh mint. We get young birds from Ashley Farms, which is a large poultry group in North Carolina raising all-natural Poulet Rouge Fermier–style birds. Poulet Rouge Fermier refers to the breed and also to the style in which they are raised, totally naturally, resulting in what most people consider to be the best eating chicken in the world.

To me it's just a little chicken done right.

I would serve this with Ramp Gratin (page 228) in the spring, Succotash (page 226) in the summer, Roasted Potato Salad (page 232) in the fall, and Cardoon Gratin (page 220) in the winter.

GRILLED POUSSIN with lemon, mint and soy

3 tablespoons olive oil

2 tablespoons soy sauce

1 tablespoon Dijon mustard

1 teaspoon grated lemon zest

1 tablespoon freshly squeezed lemon juice

¼ teaspoon red pepper flakes

2 tablespoons minced fresh mint

2 tablespoons minced fresh flat-leaf parsley

4 semiboneless poussins (available from specialty butchers)

½ teaspoon kosher salt

Prepare a charcoal or gas grill that is going to give you a medium-high heat for 10 to 12 minutes of cooking time. If you use charcoal, make sure you get the coals very gray and cooked down. This will prevent flare-ups when you cook the birds.

In a small bowl, combine the olive oil, soy, mustard, lemon zest, lemon juice, red pepper flakes, mint, and parsley. Set aside.

Place the poussins on a rimmed baking sheet and season with the salt. Slather half of the lemon-soy marinade over the poussins. Reserve the other half of the marinade for just before serving.

Wrap up 4 bricks in heavy foil. Place the birds breast side down on the grill and perch a brick on each one to weigh the chicken down and help it cook evenly. Cook for 6 minutes and then turn over the birds, lose the bricks, and cook for another 6 minutes, or until the internal temperature reads 165°F.

Transfer the cooked birds to a platter and drizzle with the remaining lemon-soy marinade.

SERVES 4

One-pot dishes are all about planning well and laying out your prep in a smart sequential order. The beauty of this dish is the vinegar, which is malty, nutty, and nuanced. I love a Philippine cane vinegar called Datu Puti. Great stuff, super-inexpensive, and readily available at most Asian grocery stores.

CANE VINEGAR CHICKEN with pearl onions, orange & spinach

• •

Season the thighs with the salt and pepper.

In a wide, heavy-bottomed pot that has a lid, melt the butter over medium heat. Add the thighs, skin side down, and let them cook without moving them around for 7 minutes. You are encouraging good caramelization of the skin and developing a ton of flavor in the process. After 7 minutes turn the thighs over and add the onions, paprika, and garlic to the pot. Cook for 5 minutes and then add the vinegar, being careful not to let it flame up.

This is a good time to get a spatula and loosen up all of those pan drippings. The vinegar needs to cook down by half, and when it does, add the stock. Cover and reduce the heat to low. Cook for 20 minutes over low heat, remove the lid, and add the oranges, mint, and spinach. Stir lightly and serve immediately.

SERVES 2 AS A BIG MAIN COURSE OR 4 AS A SMALL ONE

4 chicken thighs, each weighing 5 to 6 ounces (total of 2½ pounds chicken thighs)

½ teaspoon sea salt

¼ teaspoon freshly ground black pepper

2 tablespoons unsalted butter

16 pearl onions, peeled

¼ teaspoon smoked hot paprika

3 garlic cloves, thinly sliced

1 cup cane vinegar

1 cup Chicken Stock (page 179)

2 large navel oranges, cut into supremes (see photo, page 81)

1 tablespoon fresh mint leaves

2 cups cleaned spinach (stems removed)

AN ODE TO VINEGAR

Vinegar gets a bad rap. For starters, the name means "sour wine". The phrase "full of piss and vinegar" never meant anything good. Also, being a household cleaner never leads to gastronomic praise. There is so much more to vinegar than all of this.

To me it's all about being sour and sweet at the same time. If you add vinegar to a hot pan of roasting chicken thighs it will permeate the meat, reduce down, and give a sweet, tangy finish that is utterly delicious. A wisp of cider vinegar on wilted frisée before a poached egg goes on top balances the egg's richness. The zip of champagne vinegar in a mignonette for a perfect Chincoteague oyster provides a foil for the saline sweetness of the oyster and makes it even more alive. A drizzle of thick, unctuous balsamic over local berries in the summer provides a two-ingredient dessert perfectly balanced between sweet and sour. A cane vinegar from the Philippines in a simple vinaigrette for grilled skirt steak gives a sweet, nutty, lingering maltiness.

Without a doubt, vinegar is a rabble-rouser and wants to be the center of attention, but you do the casting in your kitchen and should thus place the vinegar where it belongs. It can learn nuance, it can even slow-dance; but you need to lead.

Vinegar has earned its place as a culinary staple.

CHICKEN BOG

2 tablespoons vegetable oil

1 chicken, cut into breasts, drumsticks, oysters, and thighs, skin removed

¼ pound andouille sausage, diced

½ cup finely chopped mixed giblets

1 bay leaf

1 leek, white and light green part, cleaned (see Note page 242) and diced (½ cup)

½ cup diced yellow onion

½ cup diced celery

½ cup diced red bell pepper

2 garlic cloves, minced

1 teaspoon chopped fresh thyme

¼ cup red wine

4 cups Chicken Stock (recipe follows) reduced to 2 cups

1 cup beef stock (see page 200)

1 large ripe tomato, peeled and diced

1 tablespoon minced fresh flat-leaf parsley

¼ teaspoon kosher salt

HMD seeks FWR.

Hearty meat dish seeks fluffy white rice.

I don't think it's just a crush. Chicken stews love rice. It's an affinity that needs to happen. Let's not sully the relationship with overly complex rice. Simply steamed rice is the key. The trick is to develop flavor with the initial browning of the meat and then add the stock slowly to encourage the stock to cook down and concentrate the flavor.

This recipe calls for a chicken with giblets, which until recently was the only way you could get a chicken. Sometime in the last decade the colonels of the chicken industry decided that we didn't deserve the giblets anymore because most of the buyers were ignorant to the goodness of the liver, neck, heart, and gizzards. Not us, though. Those little innard gems provide the flavor we need for this wonderful dish.

When we butcher chicken sometimes we neglect two glorious morsels of dark meat on the back side of the bird, right behind the thigh joint. The oysters, as they are known, are a prized little bite and shouldn't be left to the stock bones.

Heat the oil in a large, wide 6-quart pot over medium-high heat. Brown the chicken breasts, drumsticks, oysters, and thighs evenly, about 3 minutes on each side, removing them to a platter when they are nicely browned.

To the pot, add the sausage and the giblets and cook until well browned. Remove to the platter. Discard all but a tablespoon of the cooking oil and add the bay leaf, leeks, onion, celery, bell pepper, garlic, and thyme. When the onions have just turned translucent, add the red wine and reduce until almost dry.

Add the reduced chicken stock and bring to a boil. Add the reserved chicken and sausage-giblet mixture, reduce to a simmer, cover, and cook until the chicken is just done, 20 to 25 minutes. Remove the chicken pieces from the pot, pull the meat from the bones, and return it to the pot along with the beef stock. Simmer for about 15 minutes, stirring all the while to break the chicken into threads. Stir in the tomato and parsley. Discard the bay leaf. Season with the salt. Serve with rice!

SERVES 4

CHICKEN STOCK

MAKES 2 QUARTS

If you buy whole chickens you get so much from it. You get the drumsticks, thighs, oysters, breasts, giblets, and a wonderful carcass for making stock. This stock recipe doesn't have carrots in it, though I love carrots. The trouble is that the carrots get cooked too much and give a vegetal taste to the pureness of the stock, and omitting them avoids that. Make sure to skim the stock judiciously of impurities, that oily scum that rises to the top of the stock as it slowly cooks.

A 6- to 10-quart heavy stockpot is essential. Good pots are an investment, one that you can give to your children if they are nice to you. A large strainer is essential for stock making as well. Think what these investments will bring: homemade stock to pursue great soups, sauces, stews, and braises. Continue!

1 chicken carcass, chopped into 4 pieces
1 yellow onion, diced
4 celery stalks, cut into 1-inch lengths
2 large tomatoes, chopped
Bouquet garni of leek leaf, parsley, thyme, and bay leaves (see drawing, page 99)
4 black peppercorns

Rinse and pat dry the chicken carcass. Place the carcass in a large stockpot and then add the onion, celery, tomatoes, the bouquet garni, and the peppercorns. Cover all this with cold water, going over the chicken carcass by 2 inches. They kind of float but you get the idea.

Bring the pot to a boil and then simmer over low heat. Cook for 2 hours, skimming the top for fat and scum throughout the cooking time. After 2 hours, strain, discard the solids, and let the stock come to room temperature before storing in clean containers, tightly sealed, in the fridge. You can freeze stock for later use.

BRUNSWICK STEW

½ cup vegetable oil

4 chicken thighs, bone in

4 rabbit legs, bone in

1-pound piece of boneless pork shoulder, cut into 1-inch dice

½ teaspoon salt

1 cup all-purpose flour

½ pound slab bacon, minced

1 cup minced Vidalia onion

1 cup minced celery

½ pound andouille sausage, sliced

3 cups Chicken Stock (page 179)

1 cup fingerling potatoes, cut into ¼-inch discs

2 cups freshly cut corn kernels, white preferable

3 large tomatoes, peeled, seeded, and cut into ¼-inch dice

1 tablespoon tomato paste

3 garlic cloves, minced

1 teaspoon unpacked light brown sugar

1 tablespoon Worcestershire sauce

¼ teaspoon cayenne

1 teaspoon freshly squeezed lemon juice

1 tablespoon minced fresh flat-leaf parsley

1 teaspoon minced fresh thyme

1 teaspoon minced fresh rosemary

1 teaspoon minced fresh oregano

Hot Pepper Vinegar (page 265)

The hunter's larder in the South is not so full of squirrel and possum as it once was, not for lack of the little critters, but more from urbanization. City laws usually frown on hunting the squirrels in your backyard. That said I have never actually eaten squirrel and can't honestly say that I long for it. Brunswick stew is the Southern equivalent with a panoply of ingredient options, from rabbit to pork to chicken or other fowl.

Best served over rice.

Add the oil to a large pot and place over medium-high heat. Season the chicken, rabbit, and pork with the salt and then dredge in the flour. Shake off the excess flour and add the meats to the hot oil. Crisp off for 3 minutes and then turn and crisp off the other sides of the meats for 3 more minutes. Remove the chicken, rabbit, and pork from the pan and discard the hot oil.

Place the bacon in the same pot and return to medium-high heat. Cook for 5 minutes and then add the onion, celery, and andouille. Cook for 5 minutes. Return the chicken, rabbit, and pork to the pot and add 1 cup of the chicken stock. Cook down by half and then add the remaining 2 cups of chicken stock. Cover and reduce the heat to a simmer. Cook for 30 minutes and then remove the meats from the pan, leaving the liquid in the pot. Turn off the heat for the time being.

Add the fingerling potatoes, corn, and tomatoes to the pot. Cook for 10 minutes and then add the tomato paste, garlic, brown sugar, Worcestershire sauce, cayenne, and lemon juice. Cook for 15 minutes. While this is cooking, pull the meat from the chicken and rabbit bones and discard the bones. Return the chicken meat, rabbit meat, and pork cubes to the pot and cook for 15 minutes over medium heat. If the stew looks too thick you can always thin with a touch of water. Finish with the parsley, thyme, rosemary, and oregano. Serve with the hot pepper vinegar and rice.

SERVES 12

I love the little birds. Quail are versatile poultry and can be a great appetizer or a hearty main course. The quail we use at my restaurants is usually from Plantation Quail in Greensboro, Georgia, about thirty miles from Athens. It's a big outfit but they raise quail in a humane and natural way. Another popular choice around here is to go and hunt your own.

This is a truly simple recipe, but it really turns out an excellent dish.

BRAISED QUAIL with Leeks, dates, and cider

4 quail, feathered, head off, feet off, gutted and cleaned

½ teaspoon sea salt

Pinch of freshly ground black pepper

2 small yellow onions

2 tablespoons olive oil

2 medium leeks, whites and pale green parts only, cleaned (see Note page 242) and cut into ½-inch dice

½ cup medjool dates, pitted and chopped

Bouquet garni of thyme, parsley, and bay leaf (see drawing, page 99)

1 cup hard apple cider

1 cup Chicken Stock (see page 179)

Season the quail with the salt and pepper.

Peel the onions, cut them in half, and stuff an onion half into the body cavity of each bird. Truss each bird with some kitchen twine by simply tying together the drumsticks.

In a Dutch oven or other large pot over medium-high heat, warm the olive oil to just below smoking. Gently add the quail to the oil and crisp off for about 2 minutes on each breast side and then on the back. Remove the quail from the pot and set aside. Reduce the heat to medium.

Add the leeks to the pot and sweat them down for 5 minutes and then add the dates, bouquet garni, and cider. Cook down the cider for 3 minutes and then add the chicken stock and the quail. Cover and reduce the heat to a bare simmer. Cook for 15 minutes, or until quails are very tender and light brown. Serve.

SERVES 4

FRIED QUAIL BREASTS WITH CELERY ROOT SKORDALIA & POMEGRANATE SALAD

In this recipe, you will find the flavors of Greece matched perfectly with the beauty of this little bird. Skordalia is typically made with potato but in this recipe the starch is provided by cooked celery root. The celery root pairs so well with the pomegranate. Our climate in Georgia is not that similar to the climate of the Mediterranean, but pomegranate trees seem to do pretty well here. I have a friend, Jim Fiscus, who brings me grocery bags full of the beautiful red orbs. He is an award-winning professional photographer and has taken the most beautiful photographs of pomegranates, which grace the walls of my Atlanta restaurant, Empire State South.

4 semiboneless quail, each cut in half

½ teaspoon kosher salt

1 cup corn or canola oil, for frying

1 cup buttermilk

2 cups all-purpose flour

½ tablespoon pomegranate molasses

½ tablespoon freshly squeezed lemon juice

1 tablespoon extra-virgin olive oil

1 teaspoon chopped fresh mint

½ cup pomegranate seeds

1 cup fresh spinach, washed, dried, and cut into ½-inch-wide strips

½ cup Celery Root Skordalia (recipe follows)

Season the quail with ¼ teaspoon of the salt.

Heat the oil in a deep cast-iron skillet to 325°F. Dip the quail halves into the buttermilk and then into the flour, shaking any excess flour from them. Gently immerse into the hot oil and fry for about 4 minutes and then carefully turn them over and fry for another 4 minutes. Remove from the heat and place on a cooling rack.

Make a vinaigrette by combining the pomegranate molasses, lemon juice, olive oil, mint, and the remaining ¼ teaspoon of salt in a Mason jar. Seal and shake to lightly emulsify. Place the pomegranate seeds and the spinach in a medium bowl and dress with the vinaigrette.

Place a dollop of skordalia on each of 4 plates and then place two quail halves on top of each dollop. Finish with ¼ cup of the pomegranate salad on each quail.

Serve immediately.

SERVES 4

CELERY ROOT SKORDALIA

MAKES 3 CUPS

4 large garlic cloves, peeled
½ cup olive oil
2 cups peeled and cubed
    celery root
¼ teaspoon kosher salt
¼ cup roasted walnut halves
2 tablespoons freshly
    squeezed lemon juice

Place the garlic in a very small pot over low heat and cover with the olive oil. Gently poach the garlic until tender, 30 to 40 minutes. Remove from the heat and strain the garlic from the oil, reserving both separately for later use.

Cover the celery root with water in a small pot and bring to a boil. Season the celery root with the salt. Cook for 15 to 20 minutes, or until the celery root is tender. Strain the celery root and place the cubes on a rimmed baking sheet to dry out a bit.

Place the celery root, walnuts, lemon juice, and reserved garlic cloves in a food processor and blend. With the motor running add the reserved olive oil in a slow, steady stream. When the oil has been incorporated, turn off the food processor and scrape the skordalia into a medium bowl and season to taste. The skordalia should have the consistency of a thick dressing. Don't be afraid to thin it down with some water if need be.

Duck Choucroute Garnie

Choucroute garnie means "dressed sauerkraut" and is a benchmark of Alsatian food. Americans are more apt to have sauerkraut on a ballpark hot dog than at a fine restaurant, but I will put this missive on the table: Sauerkraut is great eating. You can make it yourself (you must have patient family members who can deal with the scents of fermenting cabbage in the pantry) or just find a good prepared brand like Gundelsheim or Boar's Head. In a quest to make life economical, cabbage is one of our shining stars.

1 pound sauerkraut

2 tablespoons unsalted butter

1 cup thinly sliced yellow onion

½ pound slab bacon, cut into 8 pieces

¼ cup dry vermouth

¼ cup white wine (I like to use an Alsatian Pinot Blanc)

1¼ cups Chicken Stock (page 179)

¼ teaspoon caraway seeds

6 juniper berries

½ teaspoon chopped fresh thyme

2 bay leaves

1 tablespoon olive oil

4 legs of duck confit (page 77), the drumsticks cut away from the thighs, thighs left as is but drumstick meat shredded

8 new potatoes, cooked until tender, and then halved

1 fennel bulb, cored and cut into ¼-inch-thick slices

8 baby carrots, peeled and tops removed

4 scallions, cut into 3-inch lengths

2 tablespoons minced fresh flat-leaf parsley

Kosher salt

Place the sauerkraut in a large bowl, cover with cold water, and soak for 20 minutes. Drain thoroughly in a colander, using your hands to squeeze out any excess liquid. Set aside.

In a heavy 4-quart pot, melt the butter over medium heat. Cook the onions and the bacon until the onions are translucent and tender. Add the vermouth and white wine. Cook down for 15 minutes on medium heat.

Add the sauerkraut to a saucepan. Add the chicken stock, the caraway, juniper berries, thyme, and bay leaves. Reduce the heat, cover, and braise for 45 minutes over low heat.

Place a fry pan over medium heat and add the olive oil. When the oil shimmers add the duck confit drumsticks to crisp the skin for 4 minutes. When the duck is almost done add the shredded meat and crisp lightly. Remove the duck drumsticks and the shredded duck from the pan and add to the sauerkraut pot, gently setting them on the top of the braised sauerkraut. Add the potatoes, fennel, carrots, scallions, and parsley and cover. Cook for 5 minutes and then season with the kosher salt and a drizzle of olive oil. Discard the bay leaves. Serve family-style.

SERVES 4

The key to cooking duck breasts is to start them on medium heat to slowly render the fat that protects that beautiful meat. The other key is to not overcook them. This is a play on the duck with fruit mantra, but updated with the addition of frisée, a simple vinaigrette, and some great blueberries. This and a nice bottle of red Burgundy is what July should be about.

● ●

Season the duck breasts with ¼ teaspoon of the salt. Score the skin in a crosshatch pattern with a sharp paring knife. This will help render off the duck fat.

Place a large pan over medium heat and add the canola oil. When the oil shimmers add the duck breasts, skin side down. Let cook for 8 minutes and then flip and cook for 3 more minutes. The breasts should be medium rare and should have rendered off most of their fat. Remove the breasts to a plate.

Add the onions to the duck fat still on the heat and caramelize the onions for 10 minutes over medium heat, while the breasts rest.

While the onions are cooking, make the vinaigrette. Put the mustard, ginger, and sorghum in a small bowl. Slowly whisk in the olive oil and then add the cider vinegar. Season with the remaining ¼ teaspoon of salt.

Turn the onions once or twice during their cooking. You want to develop color on them but not burn them.

Place the frisée in a bowl with the blueberries and add 2 tablespoons of the vinaigrette. Toss well and season.

Thinly slice the duck and arrange evenly on 4 plates. Top the duck with some frisée and blueberries, then the onions, and dot with a little more vinaigrette on each plate.

SERVES 4

PAN-ROASTED DUCK BREASTS with blueberries, frisée, caramelized vidalias, and sorghum vinaigrette

4 large duck breasts (I like a Peking–Long Island hybrid, the most common duck at a grocery store)

½ teaspoon kosher salt

½ tablespoon canola oil

1 Vidalia onion, peeled, halved, and sliced thin with the grain

½ tablespoon grain mustard

1 teaspoon minced peeled ginger

1 tablespoon sorghum

¼ cup extra-virgin olive oil

2 tablespoons cider vinegar

2 cups frisée (curly endive)

¾ cup fresh blueberries

Prime
Cut:
the red meats

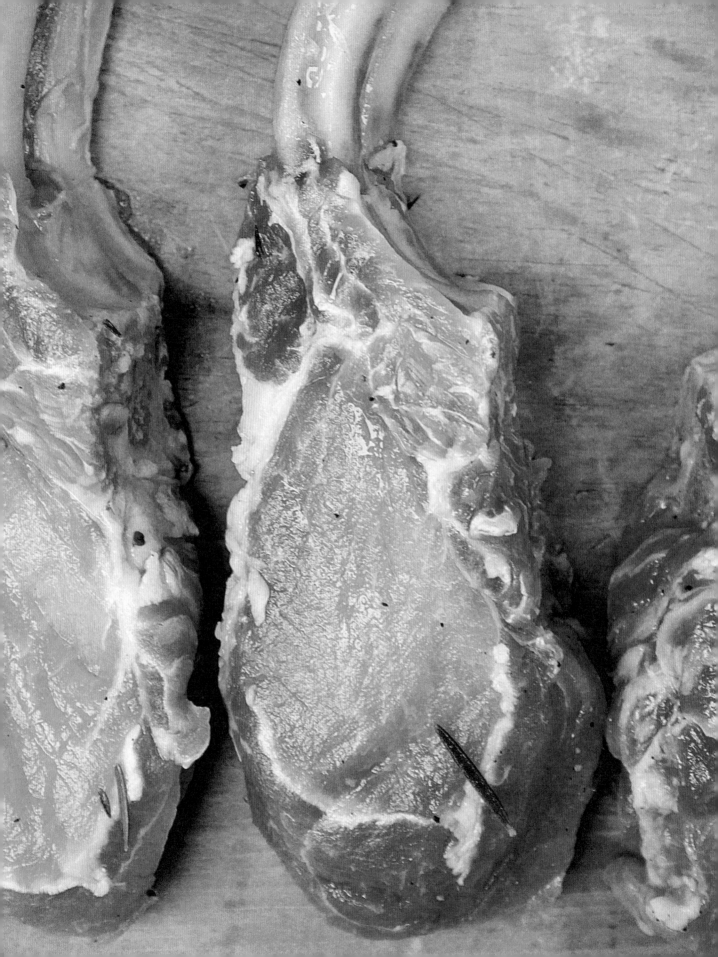

RIBEYE with stewed morels and salsa verde

braised SHORT RIBS with hominy stew

LAMB SHANKS with minted turnips

pan-roasted PORK CHOPS with baked beans
and agrodolce

smothered PORK CHOPS with chanterelles

Beef OR VEAL stock   Ham hock stock

Dads love grilling.

We had a great little grocer in Ottawa, about three blocks from home. It was called Boushey's and they had a fantastic (read expensive) butcher counter. Dad would send me there for steaks and I would pick out two rib eyes, about a pound each, bone in. Steaks are the area of the grocery store where you shouldn't be a penny pincher.

I would get back home and he would have the grill ready out back. This sequence would often take place in January when it was minus thirty degrees Fahrenheit outside. Dad loved his grill. All bundled up against the elements we'd cook those steaks and then take them inside, slice them up, and serve them with some roasted winter squash and some rice for a wonderful meal.

My time in the South has brought me more understanding of meats and their role in the Southern diet. We love pork around here and with good reason. A pig is an animal full of edible choices. It has been an animal easy to raise and easy to slaughter. It gives us bacon and ham and loin and feet. There's a lot going on there. The gospel of heritage breeds, sustainable farming, and ethical animal husbandry is making great meats a reality once again.

The following recipes are easy to accomplish but some take longer to finish. Big meat cookery takes time. It's worth it.

RIBEYE
with
STEWED MORELS
& SALSA VERDE

½ tablespoon corn oil

4 (12-ounce) rib eyes, about 1 inch thick

Kosher salt and freshly ground black pepper

1 tablespoon butter

1 sprig of fresh rosemary

1 sprig of fresh thyme

1 cup Stewed Morels (recipe follows)

4 tablespoons Salsa Verde (page 156)

I love rib eye, though at the restaurant we separate the cut into the deckle steak and the eye of rib eye. For this recipe we will use the regular cut with the deckle still intact. I say regular but I want you to go out and buy the most awesome piece of rib eye that you can afford. Prime would be great. Local dry aged would be even better. High choice would work. Angus, too. Stay away from select and watch out for anything super-inexpensive. Steak is one of those things for which great deals are just not common.

The beauty of rib eye is that it has fat, and fat is good in steak. Remember, everything in moderation. Cooking these steaks in a nice cast-iron pan harks back to the good old days. I love cast iron; it's something to care for and pass through the generations. If you see someone scrubbing your cast iron with soap and steel wool, hit them over the head with it.

Preheat the oven to 400°F.

Turn on your exhaust fan. If you don't have an exhaust fan then you should grill outdoors. Heat a large cast-iron fry pan over medium-high heat and add the corn oil. Season the steaks with salt and pepper and then add them to the pan. Sear them for about 3 minutes and then turn. Don't "flip" them, as hot oil and heavy steaks tend to create nice splashes that burn.

Cook the steaks for about 3 minutes on the second side, turn once more, and then place the pan in the oven for 4 minutes. The internal temperature should read 123°F for rare to mid-rare. Remove from the oven and add the butter, rosemary, and thyme to the pan. When the butter melts, baste by spooning it over the steaks repeatedly. This will give the meat a blanket of butteryness that makes life livable . . .

Remove the steaks and place them on a clean cutting board. Lay out 4 plates. Place ¼ cup of morels on each plate, top the morels with one rib eye, and drizzle each with 1 tablespoon of salsa verde. Serve.

SERVES 4

STEWED MORELS

2 tablespoons unsalted butter, plus more to taste
¼ cup minced shallots
2 cups fresh morels, cleaned and cut into ⅓-inch rounds
1 tablespoon sherry vinegar
¼ teaspoon minced fresh thyme
¼ teaspoon minced fresh flat-leaf parsley
¼ cup Chicken Stock (page 179)
Kosher salt and freshly ground black pepper

Melt the butter in a large fry pan and let it bubble and froth. Add the shallots and sweat down for about 3 minutes, and then add the morels. Morels, like any mushroom, will give off liquid and you want that to happen. The key is to have the pan hot enough that the morels brown, so they don't just steam in their own juice. Mushrooms carry a lot of water and when they are too close to one another they steam instead of brown.

When the mushrooms are nicely cooked, deglaze with the vinegar, add the thyme and parsley, and cook down for 4 minutes. Then add the chicken stock and stew down to the desired consistency. You can finish with a touch of butter if you want the richness to be more intense.

Short ribs are the comfortable recliner of braising. I liven them up with rich hominy stew featuring tomatoes, leeks, and roasted chiles. You can find great canned hominy at most Hispanic grocery stores or well-stocked grocers.

● ●

Preheat the oven to 325°F.

On a large plate, lay out the short ribs and evenly rub with salt and pepper. Heat a cast-iron Dutch oven over medium-high heat (if you do not have a Dutch oven you can sear in a cast-iron skillet, and transfer to a casserole dish with a lid for braising). Add the olive oil and sear all sides of the short ribs for 2 minutes per side. Make sure the hood vent is turned on before searing; this process is smoky!

Add the onion, carrot, and celery. Reduce the heat to medium and cook for 2 minutes, stirring occasionally.

Add the chile, bay leaves, thyme, and red wine. Cook to reduce the wine by about half.

Add the beef stock and bring to a light simmer. Cover and place in the preheated oven. Allow to cook for 3 to 3½ hours or until the meat is starting to pull away from the bone.

Remove the short ribs from the Dutch oven. Place them on a large plate and set aside. Using a fine-mesh strainer, strain the braising liquid into a 2-cup or larger measuring cup and discard the onion, carrot, celery, bay leaves, and thyme. Skim all of the fat off of the surface. If there is less than 2 cups of the braising liquid, add enough water to bring it up to 2 cups.

Drain and rinse the hominy. Set aside.

Lightly heat a 2-quart or larger soup pot. Add the butter, leek, and garlic. Sweat the vegetables while occasionally stirring for 4 minutes. Add the roasted green chiles, the tomato, cumin, thyme, and the 2 cups of braising liquid. Simmer for 5 minutes. Season with salt to taste.

Add the hominy and cook for another 5 minutes. Add the short ribs to reheat, spooning the stew over them as they simmer for 5 more minutes.

Turn off the heat and stir in the parsley. Ladle the stew into 4 bowls, nestling the short ribs on top.

SERVES 4

braised SHORT RIBS with hominy stew

4 (6-ounce) portions short ribs, trimmed of connective tissue

Kosher salt and freshly ground black pepper

1 tablespoon olive oil

1 medium sweet onion, peeled and coarsely cut into large dice

1 large carrot, peeled and cut into 1-inch dice

1 celery stalk, peeled and cut into ½-inch dice

1 dried ancho chile

2 bay leaves

1 sprig of fresh thyme

1 cup dry red wine

3 cups beef stock (see page 200) or store-bought beef broth

2 cups canned hominy

2 tablespoons unsalted butter

1 leek, cleaned (see Note page 242) and cut to ½-inch dice

2 garlic cloves, peeled and thinly sliced

2 tablespoons canned roasted green chiles

1 pound fresh tomato, peeled, seeded, and cut to ½-inch dice

½ teaspoon freshly ground cumin seeds

1 teaspoon chopped fresh thyme

1 tablespoon chopped fresh flat-leaf parsley

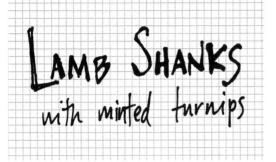

LAMB SHANKS
with minted turnips

6 (¾- to 1-pound) lamb hind shanks trimmed of excess fat

2½ teaspoons kosher salt, plus more to taste

1 teaspoon freshly ground black pepper

3 tablespoons corn oil

2 leeks, cleaned (see Note page 242) and chopped

2 medium-sized carrots, peeled and chopped

2 celery stalks, chopped

1 fennel bulb, trimmed and chopped

3 garlic cloves, minced

Bouquet garni of rosemary, thyme, and bay leaf (see drawing, page 99)

1 pound chopped and seeded tomatoes

1 cup red wine (good enough to drink)

1 quart veal stock (see page 200)

2 pounds baby turnips, unpeeled, trimmed, and finely sliced

3 tablespoons Shallot-Thyme Vinaigrette (page 111)

2 tablespoons chopped fresh mint

1 teaspoon finely sliced fresh chives

⅛ teaspoon ground cumin seeds

If getting really good at cooking is like building a house, then this is a foundation wall of a recipe. Braising is so important to really grasp and understand. Braising means to sear a protein and then to cook it in a sealed, moist environment. It breaks down tough muscles into fork-tender goodness. Patience is required, but in this regard patience is time to do the laundry list of other things while the lamb just hangs out and does its thing. What results is a meal of substance that comforts and warms you and your guests.

Jamison Lamb is a favorite of mine. From the grass pastures of Latrobe, Pennsylvania, best known for Rolling Rock beer, John and Sukey Jamison raise some of the most exquisite young lamb in the country. It melts in your mouth. I like to braise with hind shanks that weigh about 1 pound each. Fore shanks are just a bit too lean for a rich braise.

The turnips are small and tender ones—about the size of golf balls—not the waxy, gnarled ones the size of baseballs. Young, tender turnips, particularly the Hakurei varietal, are a popular local crop with our organic growers. Don't throw away those greens and stems!

Preheat the oven to 325°F.

Heat a large shallow pot (3 gallons or larger) with a lid under a well-ventilated hood over medium heat. Season the shanks evenly with 2 teaspoons of the kosher salt and the pepper. Add the corn oil to the hot pot and just before the oil is hot enough to smoke, carefully add the shanks. Make sure to allow the shanks time to brown nicely before turning. Get nice color on all sides of the shanks, then remove the shanks from the pot and place them onto a large plate. Drain off any excess oil remaining in the pot and return to low heat. Add the leeks, carrots, celery, fennel, and garlic and sauté the vegetables for 2 minutes. Return the shanks to the pot and add the bouquet garni, the seeded tomatoes, and the red wine. Let the wine reduce by half and add the veal stock, bringing it to a low simmer. Cover the pot and place in the oven for 3 hours (the meat should easily fall from the bone).

Bring 3 quarts of water to a hard boil in a 1-gallon or larger pot. Quickly submerge the turnips for 30 seconds and then immediately submerge in ice water. Drain completely and put into a large bowl with the shallot-thyme vinaigrette, ½ teaspoon kosher salt, the chopped mint, chives, and cumin seeds. Allow the turnips to soak up the flavors of the vinaigrette, herbs, and cumin at room temperature while the lamb is in the oven.

Once the lamb is tender, carefully remove and set aside on a large platter. Strain the braising liquid (using a fine conical strainer, or chinois) into a small sauce pot and bring to a simmer. As the liquid simmers, oil and rendered lamb fat will collect on the top of the liquid. With a small ladle skim the fat and discard, continuing until no more fat collects. Reduce liquid to 2 cups. Season to taste with kosher salt.

Serve the shanks on a large platter, topping them with the reduced braising liquid and the minted turnips.

SERVES 6

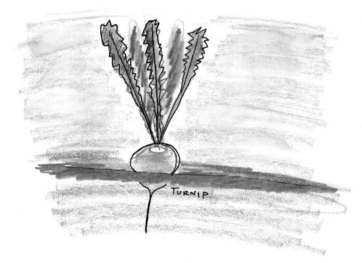

TURNIP

hindshank foreshank

PAN·ROASTED PORK CHOPS with baked beans and agrodolce

2 cups apple juice

¼ cup kosher salt

¼ cup sorghum or maple syrup

3 tablespoons coarsely ground black pepper

½ cinnamon stick

6 (1½-inch-thick) center-cut pork loin chops, trimmed of excess fat

1 tablespoon olive oil

Kosher salt and freshly ground black pepper

Baked Beans (page 219)

6 tablespoons Agrodolce (recipe follows)

Good-quality olive oil, for drizzling

For this dish you need to start brining your pork chops the day before. These chops are best over warm baked beans, which also need to be started a day before you would like to serve them.

● ●

Place the apple juice, 3 cups water, the salt, sorghum, pepper, and cinnamon in a pot and bring to a simmer. As soon as the salt has completely dissolved into the liquid turn off the heat and let the brine cool.

Place the pork chops in the brine and refrigerate for 24 hours. After the 24-hour period, remove from the brine and pat dry. Discard the brine.

Preheat the oven to 400°F.

Place a large cast-iron skillet on the largest burner and turn it to medium-high heat. Add the olive oil and let the oil warm but not smoke. Season the pork chops with salt and pepper and carefully place them in the pan. Sear for 3 minutes per side. The chops should have some nice caramelization going on and your house should be smelling awesome. Your smoke detector is probably going off, too; mine always does. If you can't fit all the pork chops in the pan then do three at a time and put them on a rimmed baking sheet.

After you've seared the chops, place them in the oven for 8 minutes.

Place a small serving of the baked beans on each plate. Then place the pork chop on top of the beans and spoon 1 tablespoon of the agrodolce on each. Drizzle with olive oil and eat away.

SERVES 6

recipe continues ⟶

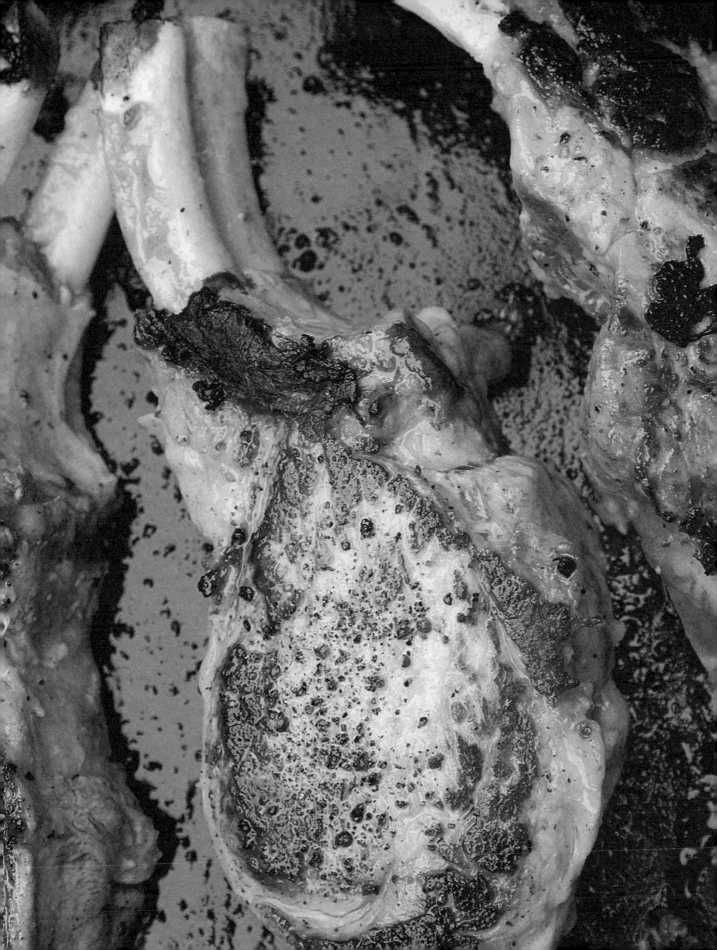

AGRODOLCE

MAKES 1½ CUPS

The agrodolce can be made up to two days in advance. Keep in a closed jar in the fridge.

2 large red bell peppers
1 tablespoon olive oil
¼ cup raisins
¼ cup port

1 tablespoon chopped fresh flat-leaf parsley
1 tablespoon balsamic vinegar
Kosher salt and freshly ground black pepper

Preheat the oven to 450°F.

Gently rub the bell peppers with the olive oil. Roast in the oven for about 15 minutes, until the peppers are blistering. Use tongs to remove the peppers from the oven and place them in a big bowl. Cover immediately with plastic wrap and let cool. This will help the skins come off easily.

Skin the peppers and discard the seeds and stalk. Chop the roasted pepper flesh into rough ½-inch dice and place in a clean mixing bowl.

Put the raisins, port, and 2 tablespoons water into a small pot and gently plump the raisins over medium heat on the stovetop for about 5 minutes. The raisins will plump up and be nice and juicy.

To the reserved chopped peppers add the plumped raisins, parsley, and balsamic vinegar. Season with salt and pepper and toss to combine.

As we have become more health-aware in the past few decades, many have tweaked what culinary smothering means. For this recipe, the pork chops are smothered in a new gravy composed of a lighter sauté of mushrooms with a touch of butter and lots of herbs.

If your meat thermometer seems wonky you can easily calibrate it by bringing a pot of water to a vigorous boil. The reading should be 212°F and if it's not you can adjust the thermometer by using a pair of pliers to turn the screw that sits just in front of the gauge housing.

* *

Preheat the oven to 400°F.

Heat a large fry pan (large enough to comfortably fit the pork chops) over medium-high heat. Lay out the pork chops onto a large plate and season with ½ teaspoon of the salt and all the pepper. Add the olive oil to the heated fry pan. When the oil is almost smoking, carefully add the chops and allow them to brown. Remove the chops from the fry pan and place them on a roasting rack over a roasting pan. Place the chops in the oven. The chops will need about 7 minutes in the oven to reach the desired internal temperature of 150°F.

While the pork chops are finishing, place a large saucepot over medium-high heat and melt the butter. When the butter beings to bubble and froth, add the chanterelles and cook for 5 minutes and then add the flour and cook for 1 minute more. Add the chicken stock by pouring it slowly while whisking continuously to prevent clumping. Turn down the heat to low and cook the stock down by half to thicken the mushroom jus into a gravy. This should take about 2 minutes. Add the thyme and remove from the heat. Whisk in the crème fraîche and lemon juice and season with the remaining ½ teaspoon of salt.

Check the chops by using an accurate meat thermometer (in the center of the thickest chop closest to the bone) to determine the temperature.

Allow the chops to rest for 5 minutes before serving. Arrange the chops onto a large rimmed platter and pour the chanterelle gravy over top.

SERVES 4

smothered PORK CHOPS with CHANTERELLES

4 (6-ounce) pork chops, bone in

1 teaspoon kosher salt

1½ teaspoons freshly ground black pepper

2 tablespoons olive oil

2 tablespoons unsalted butter

1 cup cleaned and sliced chanterelles

1 tablespoon all-purpose flour

1½ cups Chicken Stock (page 179)

1 teaspoon chopped fresh thyme

1 tablespoon crème fraîche

1 tablespoon freshly squeezed lemon juice

BEEF or **VEAL STOCK**

1 tablespoon olive oil

5 pounds beef or veal bones, cut by the butcher into manageable 3-inch pieces

1 large yellow onion, quartered

2 large carrots, scrubbed and cut into 2-inch lengths

3 celery stalks, cut into 3-inch lengths

4 roma tomatoes, halved

1 cup red Bordeaux wine

4 quarts cold water

Bouquet garni of a 6-inch leek, 1 sprig of fresh thyme, 1 bay leaf, and parsley stems (see drawing, page 99)

1 head of garlic

Do-it-yourself kitchen steps are awesome ways to slowly wean ourselves from convenience products. In no way am I a zealot, though. You will see me using tetra-pack cartons of chicken stock in my home kitchen now and again. I realize the time constraints on us these days and sometimes it's just not realistic to make everything from scratch. But making stocks is something you should get into because it is very rewarding.

Finding good fresh bones can be challenging, but when you do you can make a double batch of stock and freeze the excess. The vegetables here are cut quite large because I don't want the vegetables to cook down to an overcooked vegetable paste before the stock is done.

* *

Preheat the oven to 400°F.

Pour the olive oil into a heavy roasting pan. Add the bones to the pan and place in the oven on the middle rack to roast for about 45 minutes. Add the onion, carrots, celery, and tomatoes to the pan and roast for 10 minutes more. Remove the roasted bones and vegetables from the oven and place them carefully in a large stockpot. Pour the fat off from the pan and discard the fat.

Place the roasting pan over low heat on the stovetop and add the wine. Scrape the pan well to get all those beautiful crispy bits that have formed during the roasting. Cook for 5 minutes, then add the wine and pan drippings into the stockpot. Cover the bones and vegetables with the cold water. Add the bouquet garni and the garlic to the pot, turn the heat to high, and bring the contents to a boil. When the boil is reached reduce to a simmer immediately. As the stock cooks, skim the top to remove fat and scum. The more you remove those impurities, the cleaner and tastier your stock will be. Cook the stock for about 4 hours and then remove the solids from the pot, strain the liquid through a large strainer into another clean stockpot, and reduce the stock by half, stirring every 15 minutes or so.

When the stock is done, let it cool and then place in the refrigerator. The next day you can remove the firm fat layer that has risen to the top and then you will have a very nice clean stock. Store the stock in an airtight container in the fridge for 3 days or in the freezer for up to 4 months.

MAKES ABOUT 2 QUARTS

This is a versatile stock to have in your freezer or fridge. It's a great base for collards, field-pea soup, or a hearty winter braise. If you can find nice plump hocks from a local smoker or a great cooperative farming group like Niman Ranch, the meat that you will pick off is a great addition to many things from potato hash to risotto to scrambled eggs!

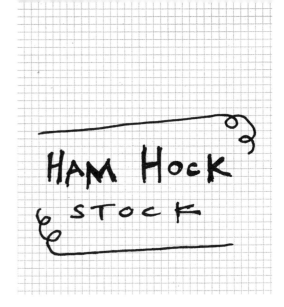

Combine the cold water and the ham hocks in a large stockpot and place over medium-high heat. Skim any foam or impurities that rise to the surface while the stock comes to a boil. Reduce the heat to a simmer and cook for 1 hour, then add the onions, celery, carrots, tomatoes, garlic, bouquet garni, and peppercorns. Cook for 1½ hours and then remove the ham hocks and strain the stock. Discard the vegetables and peppercorns. Carefully pull the good poached meat from the ham hocks, discarding the fat, bone, and connective tissue.

MAKES 3 QUARTS

4 quarts cold water

4 smoked ham hocks or 2 pounds ham trimmings, ends and pieces

2 medium onions, cut into large dice

1 heart of celery, chopped into large dice

4 carrots, coarsely chopped into large dice

2 large tomatoes, chopped

1 head of garlic, split

Bouquet garni of thyme, parsley, rosemary, and bay leaf (see drawing, page 99)

5 peppercorns

SIDES
vegetables, Grains & Taters

FLASH-COOKED OKRA with ALMONDS

NOT YOUR MAMA'S BRUSSELS SPROUTS

SHIITAKE SLAW

ARTICHOKE & SPINACH GRATIN

SQUASH CASSEROLE

GRILLED RAMPS with PECORINO, LEMON, and SEA SALT

BUTTER-BRAISED CABBAGE with CARAWAY

BAKED BEANS

CARDOON GRATIN

COLLARD GREENS

SAFFRON-BRAISED CELERY

PIQUILLO & FLAGEOLET GRATIN

SUCCOTASH

CORNMEAL CAMPFIRE TOMATOES

RAMP GRATIN

LEEK MASHED POTATOES

SORGHUM SWEET POTATOES

ROASTED POTATO SALAD

HOMINY GRITS

YELLOW GRITS

DUCK LIVER DIRTY RICE

PEPPER PILAU

HOPPIN' JOHN

RED BEANS & RICE

LEEK BREAD PUDDING

The classic Southern meal is not really that heavy on meat. It's often about choice, whether at a meat-and-three, a potluck supper, or a Sunday supper. I love being able to make up my own plate. That's where an abundance of sides makes a difference.

Sides need to be made with the freshest, best vegetables you can find. They need to shine. If you shop in season you will hit that note every time. So figuring out the seasons is key. Knowing that local tomatoes come out in July will make your menus much easier to plan. Farmer's markets have popped up around the country at a very quick pace in recent years and we need to support them. From the Ferry Building Farmers Market in San Francisco to the Union Square Greenmarket in New York City to the Virginia Highlands Market in Atlanta to the Athens Farmers Market in Bishop Park in Athens, you can find great local produce and support your local farmers pretty much anywhere.

Make some campfire tomatoes and some red beans and rice. Eat well and enjoy.

FLASH COOKED OKRA with ALMONDS

1 tablespoon olive oil

1 tablespoon cold unsalted butter

1 pound okra (stems removed and the pods cut into long pieces on the bias)

¼ teaspoon kosher salt

¼ cup sliced roasted almonds

In late summer we get beautiful pods of Louisiana green and red burgundy okra from a number of local farms. At Empire State South, I get a lot of great comments about this okra, as it conquers the problem of sludgy okra that most of us dislike. Use small pods, as the bigger they get the woodier they become. This recipe relies on high heat to cook the okra quickly and they need to be enjoyed right after you finish.

If you live in the Southeast, or in a temperate climate, consider growing your own okra as well. It's a beautiful plant with wonderful flowers.

Heat a 12-inch fry pan over high heat. Add the olive oil and butter and when the butter is melted add the okra. Sauté for 3 minutes and then season with salt and add the almonds. Toss well and remove to a platter. Serve immediately.

SERVES 4

Brussels sprouts are the hated vegetable of my generation and I am hell-bent on changing that. The trait that everyone doesn't like is the mushiness of overcooked sprouts and that is easily avoided by coring them and then peeling off individual leaves. This is time-consuming but it's worth the effort. This dish will change the tune of the most ardent sprout hater.

• •

Prepare an ice bath for chilling the Brussels sprouts' leaves. In a large 4-quart pot, boil 2 quarts water over high heat. Season the boiling water with ¾ teaspoon of the salt and then add the sprout leaves. Blanch for 1 minute and then remove to the ice bath. Drain the leaves on a non-terry-cloth towel, making sure as little water as possible and no ice remain.

In a 12-inch sauté pan, heat the olive oil and butter until it is almost smoking and carefully put the leaves into the pan. Sauté the leaves for 4 minutes or until they have some golden coloring and crisp edges to them.

Remove the leaves from the heat and add the sherry vinegar and season with the remaining ¼ teaspoon of salt. Serve immediately.

SERVES 6

NOT YOUR MAMA'S *Brussels Sprouts*

1 teaspoon kosher salt
1 pound Brussels sprouts, cored and then the individual leaves pulled off (see Note)
½ tablespoon olive oil
1 tablespoon unsalted butter
1 tablespoon sherry vinegar

NOTE: I use a small bird's-beak knife to core the sprouts. Just work the knife along the core in a circular movement and then pull it out. Repeat with all the sprouts and then remove the individual leaves. Pretend you're a GIANT working on cabbages.

I love shiitakes. They are the best non-foraged mushrooms I can rely on throughout the year. Foraged mushrooms are the ones that are not farmed but grow naturally in the forest, such as chanterelles, morels, or porcinis. Those hunted mushrooms taste better to me, but they're not always available and that's when we lean on our friend the farmed shiitake. It cooks really well and has a huge flavor.

This recipe is loosely termed a slaw but contains no mayonnaise and really is a great match to anything on the table. When you cook mushrooms just don't crowd the pan too much. Crowding the pan encourages steaming and discourages even browning and caramelization.

I love this on poultry or fish or tucked into an omelette in the morning.

¼ cup olive oil

1 quart thinly sliced shiitakes (stemmed and gently packed down when measuring)

2 teaspoons cold unsalted butter

½ teaspoon kosher salt

¼ teaspoon freshly cracked black pepper

2 tablespoons Shallot-Thyme Vinaigrette (page 111)

1 tablespoon sherry vinegar

1 tablespoon chopped fresh flat-leaf parsley

1 teaspoon chopped fresh thyme

Divide the olive oil into two pans, and heat the olive oil in both pans until just before smoking. Add 2 cups of the sliced mushrooms to each pan and allow them to turn golden brown by only stirring when needed to prevent burning (about 2 minutes). Add 1 teaspoon of the butter and half of the salt and pepper to each pan and cook the mushrooms for an additional 30 to 45 seconds. Carefully strain off any excess oil from the shiitakes and put them into a medium-size mixing bowl. Add the vinaigrette, sherry vinegar, parsley, and thyme. Toss all of the ingredients and allow to marinate for 1 hour in the refrigerator before serving.

SERVES 4

ARTICHOKE & SPINACH GRATIN

Frank Stitt is a friend, but beyond that he is a mentor from afar. His reverence for ingredients and his surefire skills have made him one of the world's most lauded chefs. You would think that with all of the accolades, all the press, all the charm and skill he would get enveloped in the ego trip that befalls many. But not Frank . . . he's cooler than that and that's why we love him.

This recipe was imagined after reading Frank's book *The Southern Table.* His use of Southern staples in French food is so natural and makes for darn good eating. This is a great side to accompany a nice grilled rib eye with a simple jus.

3 tablespoons plus 1 teaspoon unsalted butter

1 medium yellow onion, minced

1½ quarts cleaned fresh spinach

3 large, fresh Globe artichokes, trimmed and cooked (see page 213), then quartered lengthwise

3 soft-boiled eggs, peeled and cubed

½ teaspoon chopped fresh thyme

1 tablespoon chopped fresh flat-leaf parsley

1 cup Leek Crema (recipe follows)

¼ teaspoon freshly grated nutmeg

Pinch of kosher salt

Pinch of freshly ground black pepper

¼ cup grated Parmigiano-Reggiano

¼ cup freshly toasted bread crumbs (page 228)

Preheat the oven to 375°F.

Butter a gratin dish with 1 tablespoon of the butter. Set aside.

In a large fry pan over medium heat melt 2 tablespoons of the butter. Add the onion and sweat it down for 20 minutes, or until caramelized and full of flavor. Remove the pan from the heat and set aside.

To the pan, which is off the heat but still warm, add the spinach, artichokes, eggs, thyme, parsley, leek crema, and nutmeg. Gently mix together and season with the salt and pepper. Pour into the buttered gratin dish and top with the Parmigiano-Reggiano and bread crumbs. Bake for 30 minutes, or until bubbly and heated through. Serve warm.

SERVES 6

LEEK CREMA

MAKES 1½ CUPS

1 teaspoon unsalted butter

1 leek, white part only, cleaned (see Note page 242) and minced

Pinch of kosher salt

1 cup heavy cream

In a small saucepan, melt the butter over medium heat. Add the leek and 1 tablespoon water. Cover and cook, steaming the leek for about 5 minutes, until very tender. Add the salt and cream and warm through.

Remove the saucepan from the heat, puree the mixture in a blender, and strain through a fine strainer.

How to Cook a Globe Artichoke

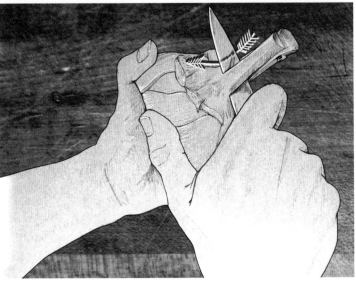

Cut in half with a serrated knife

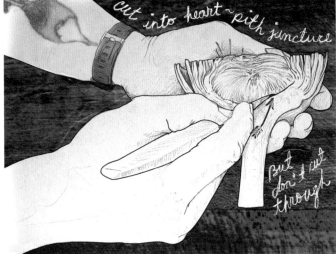

Cut into heart~pith juncture

But don't cut through

1. Trim according to the sketches you see here.

2. Place in a large pot, cover with water, and acidulate with half a lemon squeezed into the water and then the squeezed part of the lemon added to the water as well.

3. Cover with a circle of parchment paper and then weigh down with a plate that will just fit inside the diameter of the pot.

4. Place on high heat and bring to a boil, then simmer until the artichokes are tender when poked with a pairing knife—about 30 minutes.

5. Drain and let cool.

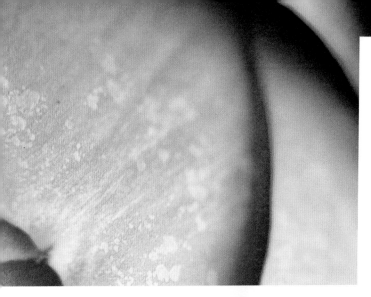

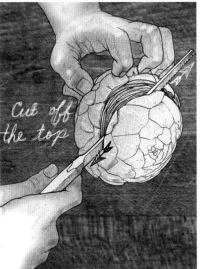

Cut off the top

Snap tough outer leaves

Pull away every thing exposing the Heart

Squash casserole is a staple of the Southern table and a really good way to use up some of that squash abundance that hits us every August. Try to find squash that is not too laden with seeds or not too water logged. Look for tight, firm squashes that look like they are the proper size and not overgrown to the point of having mushy flesh. I love Caserta, Yellow Crookneck, Black Beauty, and Cocozelle. Try your hand at growing them yourself. If I can grow them, you certainly can. I have no green thumbs but squash still comes up when I plant it.

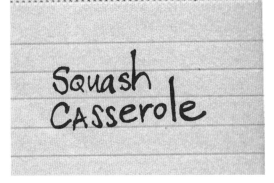

● ●

Preheat the oven to 350°F.

Coat an 8 by 10-inch casserole dish with the butter by rubbing it as if you were waxing a car. Arrange the squash in a single layer in the dish. It's all right if you shingle and overlap edges minimally. We are making a six-layer casserole, so think about that in the next few steps. We need to allocate the ingredients accordingly. Evenly coat the first level of squash with a ladle of crema, a pinch of salt, a pinch of pepper, a bit of thyme, a sixth of the bread crumbs, and a sixth of the Parmigiano. Repeat these steps five more times, and then cover the casserole with a fitted lid or foil. Bake for 25 minutes covered and 10 minutes more uncovered, or until the top becomes nice and golden brown. Allow to cool for 10 minutes before serving.

SERVES 6

1 tablespoon cold unsalted butter

3 pounds summer squash sliced lengthwise to ¼-inch-thick slices on a mandoline or with a knife

2 cups Leek Crema (page 210)

¼ teaspoon kosher salt

1 teaspoon fresh ground black pepper

1 tablespoon chopped fresh thyme

½ cup freshly made bread crumbs

½ cup grated Parmigiano-Reggiano

GRILLED RAMPS with PECORINO, LEMON, AND SEA SALT

2 teaspoons Maldon sea salt, or fine sea salt

24 wild, but clean, ramps

2 tablespoons olive oil

¼ pound Pecorino Romano, shaved with a peeler to thin strips

1 lemon

Many aromas thrill me but the scent of grilled ramps make me weep with joy. "Spring has come," it says to me. These foraged little alliums dot the Appalachians starting in late April and hang around for about three weeks. They are great pickled, made into gratins, grilled in a salad, or served simply like this.

Start a grill, preferably charcoal. The grill should take about 30 minutes to get hot and manageable. I have a Weber at home that serves us well. It isn't fancy, but that's kind of the point of charcoal grilling. If you have a gas grill, that will work too.

While the grill is getting hot, go back to the kitchen and start heating up 1 gallon of water for blanching the ramps. Once the water is rapidly boiling, add 1 teaspoon of the salt to the water.

Tie the ramps all facing the same direction. Lower the white, root end of the ramp bundle into the water and cook for 5 minutes with the white immersed but the green out of the water. While the ramps are cooking, prepare an ice bath. Remove the ramps from the water and chill them in the ice bath.

Remove the ramps from the ice bath and pat them dry with a kitchen towel. Place the ramps on a rimmed baking sheet and drizzle with a tablespoon of the olive oil. Season lightly with a pinch of sea salt.

Place the ramps on the hot grill and grill for 2 minutes per side. You want some nice charring to occur. Once grilled, remove the ramps to a platter and finish with a drizzle of the remaining olive oil, the remaining sea salt, and the Pecorino Romano. Cut the lemon in half and squeeze half of the lemon juice over the ramps.

SERVES 4

Butter-Braised Cabbage with Caraway

We could always smell rye on Boulevard Saint-Laurent, when we lived in Montreal. The bread was right out of the oven, soft in its bags, ready for a simple smear of mustard and a pile of freshly sliced ham. Lunch couldn't be simpler. Caraway is such a cool and exotic flavor and transferring it to a simple plate of cabbage is a no-brainer. This would be great with smoked meat or a wintry pork chop. Cabbage is a great value, has great vitamin properties (high in C!), and has a very low calorie count. It should be a go-to side for your dinners.

1 teaspoon caraway seeds
3 tablespoons unsalted butter
1 small yellow onion, minced
8 cups chopped Savoy cabbage
1 sprig of fresh thyme
1 bay leaf
1 cup Chicken Stock (page 179)
1 teaspoon cider vinegar
¼ cup coarsely chopped fresh flat-leaf parsley

Toast the caraway in a small, dry pan over medium heat until small wisps of smoke begin to emanate from the seeds. Pour onto a plate and set aside.

Place a large 4-quart pot over medium heat and add the butter. When it melts, bubbles, and froths, add the onion and cook for about 5 minutes, until the kitchen is filled with great beautiful aromas and the onion is wilted and beginning to color. Add the caraway and cook for 3 more minutes and then add the cabbage, thyme, and bay leaf, and stir well. Add the chicken stock and cider vinegar and cover. Cook for 20 minutes and then fold in the parsley. Serve immediately.

SERVES 4 TO 6

caraway seeds

This makes me hunger for Boston more than Macon, but this is a killer baked bean recipe. It rocks. You can also leave it in the oven for two hours or longer before you need it and it only gets better and better. Goes well with Pan-Roasted Pork Chops with Agrodolce (page 196).

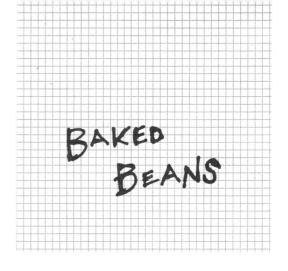

● ●

Preheat the oven to 300°F.

Strain the soaked beans and place them in a large heavy pot. Cover by 2 inches with cold water and bring to a boil, and then simmer until the beans are tender. Skim any foam that rises to the top and discard. Drain the tender, cooked beans and reserve 1 cup of the cooking liquid.

Place the cooked beans and the 1 cup of reserved cooking liquid in a heavy 3-quart baking dish or pot, with a lid. I use a really heavy enameled cast-iron pan made by Le Creuset.

Add the thyme, orange zest, garlic, dry mustard, maple syrup, and chicken stock to the beans. Arrange the bacon over the beans; cover with the lid, place in the oven, and bake for 1 hour. Remove the lid and bake for an additional 45 minutes.

Season with the salt. Serve family-style, paired with pork chops with agrodolce.

SERVES 6

2 cups white navy beans, covered in cold water and soaked for 24 hours

Cold water

1 tablespoon pulled and chopped fresh thyme

1 tablespoon minced orange zest (or use a Microplane grater)

2 garlic cloves, minced

½ teaspoon dry mustard

2 tablespoons maple syrup or sorghum

2 cups Chicken Stock (page 179)

6 slices bacon, cut into 3-inch lengths

½ teaspoon kosher salt

BAKED BEANS MAKE PEOPLE HAPPY

CARDOON GRATIN

½ lemon

12 large cardoon stalks, about 1 inch wide and 10 inches long

2 teaspoons kosher salt

3 tablespoons unsalted butter

1 medium leek (white and light-green parts), cleaned (see Note page 242), and finely diced

1 tablespoon freshly minced garlic

1½ cups heavy cream

¼ teaspoon freshly grated nutmeg

½ cup grated Parmigiano-Reggiano

½ cup freshly toasted bread crumbs

1 teaspoon minced fresh thyme

Pinch of red pepper flakes

Cardoons are a thistle. Thistles are temptingly beautiful but a bit scary looking, too. Their fibrous stalks, once cut away from the leaves and foliage, taste like an artichoke . . . lots of work to get to but oh so worth it. They have a short winter season and are definitely a vegetable that you may have to demand from your produce person, rather than just stumble on. Cardoons appear in better grocery stores and then don't show up again for a year. Ask your grocer or, if you live in a large city, then find your Little Italy and shop the stores there.

Preheat the oven to 375°F.

Fill a large bowl with cold water and squeeze the lemon half into the water, then place the whole half lemon in there, too. With a sharp peeler remove the outside layer of the cardoons and trim the ends. Pretend you're whittling down the hardiest piece of celery ever and you'll be on the right track. Cut each cleaned cardoon stalk into 2-inch pieces and place them in the water.

Remove the cardoons from the bowl of acidulated water and place them in a large pot (with a lid) of cold water. The cardoons should be in ample water to more than cover them. Cover the pot with its lid and bring to a boil. Add 1 teaspoon of the salt and reduce the temperature to a simmer. Cook for about 30 minutes, or until the cardoons are tender to the tip of a sharp knife. Strain and reserve.

Place a medium pot over medium heat and add 2 table-spoons of the butter. When it's melted, and bubbles and froths, add the leek. Sweat down the leek for 10 minutes and then add the garlic. Stir well and then let the garlic and leek cook an additional 5 minutes. Do not burn the garlic. Add the cream and nutmeg and cook for 5 minutes. Turn off the heat and reserve. Season with the remaining teaspoon of salt.

CARDOONS LOOK LIKE MENACING CELERY . . . BUT HAVE BEAUTIFUL THISTLE FLOWERS!

Get a nice heavy baking dish (I love enameled cast iron for this, such as Staub or Le Creuset) and butter it up with that last tablespoon of butter.

Pour about a quarter of the leek cream in the bottom of the baking dish. Layer cardoons and then add another quarter of the leek cream. Add half of the cheese in an even layer. Continue until all the leek cream, the cheese, and the cardoons are layered. Finish by evenly spreading the bread crumbs on the top and add the thyme and red pepper flakes.

Bake uncovered for 30 minutes, or until the cream has thickened up, the bread crumbs are toasty, the smells are awesome, and the gratin looks good enough to eat all by yourself.

SERVES 6

this is
thyme...

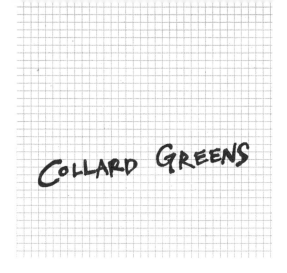

COLLARD GREENS

Collards are magnetic. You either are so attracted to them that you can't get enough or they repel you. The potlikker is the ethereal liquid that is created from that mix of smoky hock, the chicken stock, vinegar, and the great flavors that the collards give off. I save this liquid for things like Seared Day-Boat Scallops (page 159) or make it into a simple soup with chopped collards, rice, and hot sauce.

I like collards a bit smaller and younger than most grocery stores have them. The younger ones make for a much more tender green and you don't have to cook them as long. If you can find a local organic farmer who is growing collards, then buy away. You have to wash all collards really well in three changes of water, but let's ignore stories about using the washing machine or dishwasher for this task. I don't believe those tales much at all.

You need a large pot here, because the collards are going to be a huge quantity while raw and much less of one when cooked.

3 tablespoons olive oil

1 large yellow onion, minced

4 pounds cleaned collard greens, pulled into bite-size pieces

¼ cup sherry vinegar

2 tablespoons sorghum or maple syrup

4 cups Chicken Stock (page 179)

1 small smoked ham hock or hunk of slab bacon

1 teaspoon kosher salt

½ teaspoon red pepper flakes

1 tablespoon unsalted butter

Warm the oil in a large pot over medium heat, add the onion, and cook until the onion has some color.

Add the collards and sauté until they are a bit limp, 4 to 5 minutes. Add the vinegar and cook down. Add the sorghum, stock, 2 cups water, the ham hock, salt, and red pepper flakes. Cook, covered, for about 2 hours, or until the collards are tender. Add the butter and reserve warm until ready to serve.

SERVES 8

collard greens

Celery is a recession delight. The ubiquitous stock vegetable is just downright inexpensive. To most though it's a garnish for chicken wings or a bloody Mary, but not much more. The beauty of it shows through when you give it more of a starring role in your dish.

Saffron to me is something to be used sparingly because adding too much makes food taste like a savory perfume and not food. Saffron is a spice and spices need to be fresh, so unless you are embarking on a Persian-themed diet, buy saffron in very small quantities at a reputable grocery or spice dealer.

This dish is a perfect accompaniment to Gigged Flounder (page 147) or a roasted chicken, or just chopped up with Red Beans and Rice (page 240).

Saffron-Braised CELERY

2 tablespoons unsalted butter
2 shallots, thinly sliced
12 celery stalks, peeled (avoid the leafy parts, which are very assertive)
1 little pinch of saffron
1 cup Chicken Stock (see page 179)
Kosher salt and freshly ground black pepper

Preheat the oven to 350°F.

In a sauté pan over medium heat, melt the butter and sweat the shallots for about 5 minutes. You are not trying to caramelize the shallots, merely extracting their sweetness.

Cut the celery into 3-inch lengths and place them in the pot. Add the saffron and stock. Cover and braise in the oven for 30 minutes, or until tender. Season with salt and pepper to taste. Serve hot.

SERVES 4

CORN
+
TOMATO
+
BASIL

2 large ripe heirloom tomatoes

½ teaspoon kosher salt

2 cups freshly cut white corn kernels

2 tablespoons Shallot-Thyme Vinaigrette (page 111)

1 tablespoon cider vinegar

¼ cup fresh farmer's cheese or feta, crumbled

2 tablespoons chopped fresh flat-leaf parsley

12 fresh basil leaves, torn by hand into small pieces

That's all it is. And some great cheese.

I am not sure whether it should be a side or a salad but last time I had this, it was a side, so here it lies.

Raw corn, cut tomatoes, and fresh basil. This is a great side for poached chicken or a roasted fish in the middle of the summer. Raw food at its simple best.

I find Silver Queen to be the most available white corn around but if you find some nice yellow corn, continue with that by all means. As for tomatoes, you know the rules: only the most local, most beautiful, most wondrous ones will do.

Core the tomatoes and cut them into a large dice, about 1 by 1 inch.

Place the tomatoes in a large bowl, season with the salt, and let them sit for 30 minutes at room temperature.

The tomatoes will have exuded a fair bit of liquid and that is good stuff. Add the corn, vinaigrette, cider vinegar, cheese, parsley, and basil to the tomatoes. Gently mix with a spoon and serve immediately.

SERVES 4

PIQUILLO ½

FLAGEOLET

GRATIN

Piquillo peppers are fire-grilled Spanish peppers that look like small horns. They are sweet and spicy at the same time. Flageolets are beautiful beans of French origin that are wonderful in everything from a soup to a cassoulet to this gratin. Combined they make a pretty darn good side next to some lamb. If you can't find piquillos you could use roasted red peppers; if you can't find flageolets you could use Great Northern white beans. In a pinch, canned beans work pretty well; but let that be your last resort.

⚫ ⚫⚫ ⚫⚫ ⚫ ⚫⚫ ⚫⚫ ⚫ ⚫ ⚫⚫ ⚫ ⚫⚫ ⚫ ⚫⚫ ⚫ ⚫⚫ ⚫ ⚫⚫ ⚫ ⚫⚫

2 tablespoons extra-virgin olive oil

1 medium yellow onion, diced

4 garlic cloves, minced

1 cup chopped roasted piquillo peppers

1 cup chopped spinach

1 cup cooked flageolet beans, with 1 cup cooking liquid

¼ cup diced cooked bacon, not too crispy

1 tablespoon minced fresh rosemary

1 teaspoon minced fresh thyme leaves

¼ cup grated Parmigiano-Reggiano

¼ cup homemade bread crumbs (see page 228)

Kosher salt and freshly ground black pepper

Preheat the oven to 400°F.

Place a heavy pot or large cast-iron pan over medium heat. Add the olive oil and wait until it warms to just below smoking. Add the onion and cook for 5 minutes, stirring every once in a while. Add the garlic and cook for 2 minutes. Turn off the heat.

Place the cooked onions and garlic in a large bowl and add the peppers, spinach, beans, cooking liquid, cooked bacon, rosemary, and thyme. Stir with a wooden spoon to combine. Pour the mixture into a buttered 10 by 7-inch baking dish and top with the Parmigiano-Reggiano and the bread crumbs. Season with the salt and pepper to taste.

Cover with foil and bake for 30 minutes, then uncover and bake for 10 more minutes.

SERVES 6

Succotash

There will be no "sufferin' succotash" coming out of my kitchens. If field peas aren't around, you could adjust with some butter beans, lima beans, or black-eyed peas. I love dried pigeon peas or dried Sea Island red peas from coastal Georgia as well. In a seasonal pinch, frozen can work for the bean or pea element; just please don't you dare do that with the corn. Frozen corn tastes like freezer first and corn second.

So the ideal elements of succotash are: fresh peas or beans if possible, fresh corn, fresh tomato, sweet onion, basil, thyme, and chicken or ham hock stock.

1 cup fresh peas (crowder, Purple Hull, butter bean), or frozen peas in a pinch

1 ounce slab bacon, in 1 piece

½ teaspoon kosher salt

1 tablespoon olive oil

½ medium sweet onion, minced

1 leek, white and light-green parts, cleaned (see Note page 242) and minced (½ cup)

3 ears of fresh yellow corn, shucked, cut from cob, and the cobs scraped of any corn milk

1 large heirloom tomato, peeled, seeded, and finely diced

¼ cup Chicken Stock (page 179) or Ham Hock Stock (page 201)

¼ cup torn fresh basil

1 teaspoon chopped fresh thyme

1 tablespoon chopped fresh flat-leaf parsley

Place the peas, bacon, and ¼ teaspoon of the salt in a medium pot and cover with cold water. Bring to a boil and then simmer until the beans are cooked through, anywhere from 20 to 45 minutes depending on your bean choice. Drain, discard the bacon, and set the beans aside.

From this point forward it's pretty much just about blending ingredients for a fresh, seasonal result.

In a large fry pan, warm the olive oil over medium-high heat. Add the onion and leek and cook until translucent, about 2 minutes. Add the corn and tomatoes and cook for 2 minutes. Add the cooked peas and chicken stock, stir well, and cook for 2 minutes. Add the basil, thyme, and parsley. Season to taste with the remaining ¼ teaspoon of salt.

SERVES 6

Breakfast in the South often features fried green tomatoes. Breakfast in Canada often features fried red tomatoes. This recipe leans to the Canadian side but adapts well to any meal. I call them campfire tomatoes because I have a beautiful retirement dream of cooking these on a cast-iron skillet next to a stream in the mountains, eating them up with freshly caught grilled trout and a bacon vinaigrette. In my dream I am adept at wilderness living and have a handsome beard, a Mackinaw vest, and great whittling skills.

Until my dream comes true I will use my cast-iron skillet on the stove at home.

You could use any tomatoes for this, and if you made it with Brandywines or another nice homegrown heirloom, it would only get even better.

CORNMEAL CAMPFIRE TOMATOES

6 ripe tomatoes (such as roma or an heirloom variety)
½ cup yellow cornmeal
¼ cup all-purpose flour
1 teaspoon chopped fresh thyme
½ teaspoon kosher salt
¼ teaspoon freshly ground black pepper
3 tablespoons bacon fat or vegetable oil

• •

Cut off the ends of each tomato, creating flat sides on the core end and bottom. Then cut each tomato in half at the equator, making two smaller cylinders. Mix the cornmeal and flour together in a medium mixing bowl. On a plate lay out all of the tomato halves and season with the thyme, salt, and pepper. Press each tomato gently into the flour-cornmeal mixture, making sure to coat both sides. Heat a cast-iron skillet over medium heat and add the bacon fat. Add the tomatoes to the hot skillet and crisp until the tomato crust is golden brown on both sides, about 3 minutes on each side.

SERVES 4

RAMP GRATIN

½ pound ramps, raw, cleaned, and trimmed

1 teaspoon cold unsalted butter

1½ cups Leek Crema (page 210), heated to just below a simmer

¼ cup grated Parmigiano-Reggiano

½ teaspoon kosher salt

¼ teaspoon freshly ground black pepper

1 cup Herby Bread Crumbs (recipe follows)

Oh, ramps. I love them more than any other castaway of the onion family. They are the savage, wild, foraged one who was always picked last. They shine on my team, though, with their gutsy flavor and their brief seasonal appearance.

This is another gratin, a bubbly cream-driven beautiful thing. If you can't find ramps, we have made this with the more common scallions or leeks as well and had great results—but not as soulful as the ramp version.

Preheat the oven to 350°F.

Pour 1 gallon water into a large pot and bring to a rapid boil. Prepare an ice and water bath.

Tie the ramps into a bundle and for 30 seconds quickly submerge the bundle into the rapidly boiling water. Immediately submerge into the ice and water bath in order to cool the ramps instantly. Strain off any remaining water and cut the ramps into 3-inch pieces.

Rub the butter over the entire inner surface of an 8 by 8-inch pan or baking dish that is at least 2 inches deep. Arrange the ramp pieces in the pan. Pour the warm leek crema over the ramps. Sprinkle the Parmigiano, salt, pepper, and the bread crumbs evenly over the top and bake for 20 minutes or until Parmigiano is lightly browned. Allow to cool for 5 minutes before serving.

SERVES 4

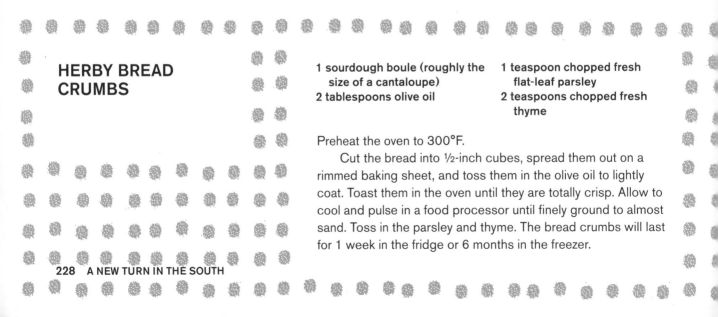

HERBY BREAD CRUMBS

1 sourdough boule (roughly the size of a cantaloupe)

2 tablespoons olive oil

1 teaspoon chopped fresh flat-leaf parsley

2 teaspoons chopped fresh thyme

Preheat the oven to 300°F.

Cut the bread into ½-inch cubes, spread them out on a rimmed baking sheet, and toss them in the olive oil to lightly coat. Toast them in the oven until they are totally crisp. Allow to cool and pulse in a food processor until finely ground to almost sand. Toss in the parsley and thyme. The bread crumbs will last for 1 week in the fridge or 6 months in the freezer.

Ramps are a spring messenger. They pop up and we rejoice that everything is warming and blooming once again. We treat them simply with a hot grill, great olive oil, some shaved cheese. We eat with gusto. You gotta love spring.

LEEK MASHED POTATOES

2 pounds russet potatoes, peeled and
    cut into 1-inch cubes

1½ teaspoons kosher salt

1 large leek, white and light-green
    parts, cleaned (see Note page 242)
    and cut into ¼-inch squares

¼ pound (1 stick) unsalted butter

½ cup heavy cream

Joël Robuchon, the esteemed French chef with outposts around the world, is the creator of the richest whipped potatoes in the culinary universe. These are not Robuchon's potatoes. This recipe is more like butter with a touch of potato. It takes the same idea but lightens it up and adds the beauty of leeks, a flavor that I never tire of. Pair this with some roasted chicken and a white Burgundy and you have a Sunday to remember.

Place the potatoes in a large pot and cover with cold water. Bring to a boil and add 1 teaspoon of the salt, then reduce the heat to medium-low to simmer the potatoes. Cook them until fork tender.

While the potatoes are cooking, sauté the leeks. Place a large fry pan over medium heat and add the butter. When the butter bubbles and froths, add the leeks and cook until translucent, about 10 minutes. Add the cream and bring to a gentle simmer.

Drain the potatoes, reserving a cup of the cooking water just in case you need to thin down the potatoes. Work the potatoes through a food mill or ricer. Gently fold the leek cream into the potatoes. If the consistency is too thick, add a touch of the potato cooking water to create the desired consistency. Season with the remaining salt, or more to taste.

SERVES 6

This simple whipped potato is a great side in the fall and belongs on your Thanksgiving table. The chile balances the sweetness of the potatoes, and the butter makes everything richer and more opulent. I left off the little marshmallows because I think we need to evolve . . . and my dentist friends would get mad at me if I used them. You can garnish sweet potatoes with a variety of flavors from cooked apples to more cooked chiles to hazelnuts or even a dollop of yogurt.

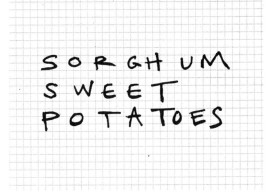

SORGHUM SWEET POTATOES

3 pounds sweet potatoes, peeled and cut into 1-inch cubes

1 teaspoon kosher salt

3 tablespoons unsalted butter

1 red jalapeño chile, minced

¼ teaspoon grated orange zest

½ cup heavy cream

¼ cup Chicken Stock (page 179)

2 tablespoons sorghum or maple syrup

¼ teaspoon freshly grated nutmeg

Place the sweet potatoes in a large pot and cover with water. Bring to a boil, season with ½ teaspoon of the salt, and cook until tender. While the sweet potatoes are cooking, melt the butter in a small saucepan and when the butter bubbles and froths, add the jalapeño and the orange zest. Cook for 1 minute, turn off the heat, and then add the cream. Set aside.

When the sweet potatoes are fork tender, drain them in a colander set up in your sink. Let them drain completely and then pass them through a ricer or mash them well with a potato masher. Add the flavored cream, chicken stock, sorghum, nutmeg, and the remaining ½ teaspoon of salt. Mix well and transfer to a nice serving bowl.

SERVES 8

ROASTED POTATO SALAD

2 pounds new or fingerling potatoes, blanched until just tender, drained, and then quartered

2 garlic cloves, peeled and smashed

1 teaspoon chopped fresh rosemary

½ pound (2 sticks) unsalted butter, cubed

¼ cup Dijon mustard

1 egg yolk

Pinch of cayenne

¼ teaspoon kosher salt

⅛ teaspoon freshly ground black pepper

½ cup extra-virgin olive oil

1 tablespoon cider vinegar

½ cup finely diced red onion

¼ cup minced red bell pepper

¼ cup minced scallions

¼ cup chopped fresh dill

Bradley Ogden doesn't know me from Adam, but that doesn't mean that he hasn't shaped the cooking I do every day. Ogden is a Bay Area chef who has been very influential with his respectful use of his local ingredients. The way I have learned to advance my cooking foundation has been to read the books and learn from the best cooks, people who have made an impact on their communities. A version of his roasted potato salad has graced many menus that I have done in the last twenty years since he published his seminal cookbook, *Bradley Ogden's Breakfast, Lunch and Dinner.* Books like that should have a place on your kitchen shelf.

Preheat the oven to 400°F.

Combine the potatoes, garlic, rosemary, and butter in a roasting pan and cover with aluminum foil. Place in the oven and bake for 10 minutes. Then, uncover the roasting pan and roast for another 10 minutes. The potatoes should have a nice, slightly golden color. Remove the pan from the oven, but keep the potatoes in the roasting pan.

In a large bowl, whisk together the mustard, egg yolk, cayenne, salt, and pepper. Add the olive oil slowly. Once it is incorporated, add the warm potatoes, cider vinegar, red onion, bell pepper, scallions, and dill to the bowl. Stir well. Season with salt and pepper.

SERVES 6

Hominy grits come to us from Anson Mills in Columbia, South Carolina. Hominy grits are ground dry corn kernels that have gone through a process of nixtamalization, or soaking in a caustic lye, which plumps them up. The resulting hominy kernel is a kitchen staple in pozole and other dishes, but dried and ground it is hominy grits. Hominy grits are richer and plumper, almost fluffy in a moist way, compared with yellow grits. They are wonderful and if you ever hear anyone dissing grits it is probably because they have been served instant grits. Instant grits are the Axis of Evil of the food world.

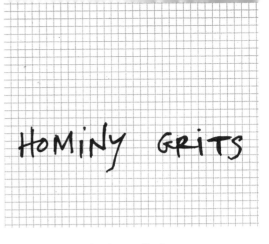

1 teaspoon kosher salt, plus more
  to taste
1 cup hominy grits
1 cup whole milk
2 tablespoons butter
Freshly ground black pepper

Place the teaspoon of salt, the grits, milk, and 3 cups water in a large saucepan over medium heat and bring to a boil. Reduce the heat to a bare simmer. Whisk for a couple minutes, reduce the heat to low, and then swap over to a wooden spoon as the grits begin to thicken up. Stir every minute or so until they're done, which is about 1½ hours. Stir in the butter and season with salt and pepper to taste. Serve warm.

SERVES 6

grits... not just for breakfast.

YELLOW GRITS

1 teaspoon salt, plus more to taste
1 cup yellow grits
1 cup whole milk
2 tablespoons butter
Freshly ground black pepper

Yellow grits are a coarser grind than polenta, and much coarser than cornmeal. Ours are ground from organic dried corn in Tim Mills's brilliantly simple grist mill that he built in 1990 from old truck parts, salvaged material, and very hard work. It is powered by a well-cared-for mule. Tim looks like a Steinbeck character with his simple overalls and beard but he relishes talking about his work and his ideas. I remember wandering the farm with him as he talked about things that have worked and things that haven't, the quality of corn that season, drying tomatoes for tomato chips, and the abundance of beautiful thin leeks that were popping up everywhere. The whole time he was busily whittling away on a small piece of wood with his old pocketknife. At the end of our chat he folded his knife and placed a perfectly crafted toothpick in his mouth. It was beautiful.

The mill was schematically rendered by a very impressed visiting mechanical engineer–artist and has now been replicated in Ethiopia to mill sorghum, a crop that is abundant oddly enough in our South and also in Africa.

When I call Alice (Tim's wife) to order some grits, I know that the mule gets to work powering the mill and Tim feeds the corn into the hopper. Talk about limiting your middlemen.

Place the teaspoon of salt, grits, 3 cups water, and the milk in a large saucepan over medium heat, and bring to a boil. Once boiling, reduce the heat to a bare simmer. Whisk for a couple of minutes, reduce the heat to low, and then swap over to a wooden spoon as the grits begin to thicken. Stir every minute or so until they're done, which is about 45 minutes. The consistency should be that of porridge, not of soup. Stir in the butter and season with salt and pepper to taste. Serve warm.

SERVES 6

I love this spicy rice dish, another ode to Louisiana and the masters of the culinary world who have cooked there. People like Paul Prudhomme, John Folse, and the late Justin Wilson ("I Gar-on-tee!") are the backbone of great Louisiana food. Now you have a new vanguard of some pretty awesome people cooking down there: Donald Link, John Besh, Susan Spicer, and John Harris.

It's cooking that you can learn something new about every day, and their opus is getting ever more beautiful.

The livers I am looking for are the ones found in regular ducks, not in foie-gras ducks, so let's leave the whole foie-gras debate alone for this one. If you can't find duck livers, you can use chicken livers, but let me be clear: The chicken livers you get in bulk at the cheapie grocery store are not the mantel you want to hang your rice on. You find great livers when you find great chickens. Search away!

Duck Liver Dirty Rice

½ tablespoon bacon fat

¼ pound ground pork

½ cup minced yellow onion

¼ cup minced celery

¼ cup minced poblano chile

3 minced garlic cloves

¼ teaspoon cayenne

¼ teaspoon freshly ground black pepper

½ teaspoon sweet smoked paprika

½ teaspoon dry mustard

¼ teaspoon ground cumin

1 tablespoon fresh thyme leaves

2 tablespoons fresh oregano leaves

3 tablespoons finely chopped duck livers

2 bay leaves

1 tablespoon unsalted butter

2 cups Chicken Stock (page 179)

1 cup basmati rice

½ teaspoon kosher salt

● ●

Place the bacon fat and ground pork in a heavy pot (with a lid) and place over medium-high heat. Cook for 10 minutes, very occasionally stirring to break up the pork. You should get some stickage going on. This is going to equate to flavor in the end.

Add the onion, celery, poblano, and garlic. Stir well to start removing some of the cooked meat specks from the bottom and cook for 5 minutes. In a small bowl, mix the cayenne, black pepper, paprika, dry mustard, cumin, thyme, and oregano. Add this blend to the pot, and stir well. Add the duck livers and cook for 2 minutes.

Add the bay leaves, butter, stock, rice, and salt. Cover and bring to a boil and then simmer for 20 minutes, or until the rice is tender. Discard the bay leaves and serve the rice.

SERVES 4 TO 6

"Call Anson Mills."

That's a simple entry on my calendar, but I should probably reserve more time than your average ordering call, because calling Anson Mills is like opening up an encyclopedia of grains steeped in Southern knowledge. Glenn Roberts is the brain and brawn behind Anson Mills and they are changing the way we eat, or at least bringing it back to days of yore. Based in Columbia, South Carolina, Glenn has become the resource for milled products that taste like they would have a hundred years ago before we had factories squeeze all the goodness out of food. If you need to know about "Carolina Gourdseed White" corn and the processes of hominy grits, Glenn is your guy.

Glenn sells a lot of Carolina Gold, a heritage long-grain rice that was a staple of the South for two hundred fifty years and then disappeared as parboiled rice took over the world. It was replanted by an ophthalmologist near Charleston as food for the fowl the doctor liked to hunt, and Glenn began producing it in 2006.

A pilau is a pilaf is a pirloo. You can vary the ingredients in this; it's the technique that carries through.

Pepper Pilau

¾ cup long-grain white rice (Carolina Gold would be great!)

½ teaspoon kosher salt

1 teaspoon extra-virgin olive oil

½ small yellow onion, minced

¼ cup finely diced bacon

2 garlic cloves, minced

1 roasted jalapeño chile, seeded and minced

½ cup finely diced roasted sweet red peppers

1 teaspoon smoked paprika

Pinch of cayenne

1 tablespoon cider vinegar

¼ cup chopped fresh flat-leaf parsley

In a small pot, combine the rice, 1½ cups water, and ¼ teaspoon of the salt. Bring to a boil, then reduce the heat to very low, cover, and cook for 20 minutes. When the rice is cooked, remove it from the heat, fluff, cover, and set aside.

Working in a medium-size stainless-steel pan or pot, warm the oil over medium heat. When the oil shimmers (before it smokes), add the onion and bacon. We are using such a small amount of oil because more fat will be rendered from the bacon. Cook for 10 minutes, stirring frequently, until the onions have some nice color and the bacon is cooked. Add the garlic, jalapeño, and red peppers and continue to cook for another 5 minutes.

Reduce the heat to low and add the paprika, cayenne, and cider vinegar. Season with the remaining ¼ teaspoon of salt and then add the parsley. Remove from the heat and add to the cooked rice. Combine well. Serve immediately.

SERVES 4

HOPPIN' JOHN

1½ cups dried black-eyed peas

1 smoked ham hock

2 bay leaves

1 cup basmati rice

¼ teaspoon kosher salt

3 tablespoons unsalted butter

1 large Vidalia onion, minced

1 cup peeled and minced celery

1 poblano chile, cored, seeded, and minced

1 medium-size red bell pepper, cored, seeded, and minced

Pinch of red pepper flakes

1 teaspoon Hot Pepper Vinegar (page 265)

Hoppin' John is the rice and beans of the South. Some people make it more into a rice salad, but here it is . . . It should be zesty and full-flavored but clean, too. I love that vinegar zip that makes things fresh.

Tradition has it that we eat Hoppin' John on New Year's Day, but I feel comfortable eating it pretty much anytime. It's so good that it deserves more than a once-a-year appearance on your table. The leftovers from Hoppin' John are called Skippin' Jenny. Those leftovers can be turned into a nice soup with some Ham Hock Stock (page 21) and fresh herbs.

Place the peas, hock, and bay leaves in a large pot and cover with cold water. You want to have enough water, so go about 2 inches over the dried peas. Place on medium-high heat and bring to a boil.

Reduce the heat to medium low, cover, and simmer for about 25 minutes, or until the peas are tender but not so far as to mush them all up. They should be tender but intact. If there is still a lot of liquid in the pot then drain it off, keeping the peas in the pot. Remove the hock from the peas and pull all the nice meat off and coarsely chop it. The bone and sinew can be discarded. Add the nice meat back to the peas.

Place the rice in a pot and add 1½ cups cold water, the salt, and 1 tablespoon of the butter. Bring to a boil, cover, and simmer over low heat for 20 minutes. Remove from the heat and then fluff with a fork before using.

While the rice is cooking, place a large fry pan over medium heat. Add the 2 tablespoons of remaining butter and let it melt, bubble, and froth. Don't brown the butter, though. Add the onion and celery and cook for 4 minutes, stirring once in a while. Add the poblano and bell pepper, reduce the heat to medium low, and continue to cook for 15 minutes, or until the flavors have really developed. Add the red pepper flakes and combine this mixture with the peas.

Now you can marry the finished rice to the finished peas and you have Hoppin' John! Finish with the hot pepper vinegar, adjust the salt, and start the new year off right!

SERVES 6

RED BEANS & RICE

½ pound dried small red beans, picked over and rinsed

½ pound smoked ham hock

1 large yellow onion, chopped

2 celery stalks, chopped

1 large red bell pepper, cored, seeded, and chopped

1 teaspoon cayenne

¼ bunch fresh flat-leaf parsley, chopped

2 sprigs of fresh thyme

3 bay leaves

4 garlic cloves, chopped

2 scallions, green part only, chopped, plus more for garnish

Red pepper sauce, such as Texas Pete

Salt and pepper to taste

4 cups cooked white rice

My dad fed us a lot of red beans and rice made with Uncle Ben's and canned beans. Let's put it this way, it matched well with the fish sticks and canned yellow wax beans. It was a balanced meal but lacked the beauty of great fresh food. This recipe takes really aromatic beans and marries them with beautiful rice to match the best of the Southern table. For the beans, I go to Rancho Gordo in Napa, California. They are raising heirloom beans and are fanatical about fresh crop beans and really cool varietals. I particularly like their Santa Maria Pinquito beans for this recipe.

Place the dried beans in a large bowl and cover with cold water. Soak the beans overnight in the refrigerator.

Drain the beans and put them in a large heavy pot with the ham hock, adding just enough cold water (about 2 quarts) to cover. Add the onion, celery, bell pepper, cayenne, parsley, thyme, bay leaves, garlic, scallions, and several shakes of red pepper sauce. Give it all a good stir to combine. Simmer, uncovered, until the beans are tender and starting to thicken, about 2½ hours. You want the beans to be fully soft and cooked, like they are getting ready to burst. Stir the beans occasionally to prevent scorching on the bottom of the pot. Add about 1 cup water toward the end of cooking if the mixture appears too thick or dry.

Mash 1 cup of the cooked beans against the side of the pot with a wooden spoon; this makes the broth thick and creamy. Season with salt and pepper, and discard the bay leaves. Serve the red beans in a wide bowl over steamed white rice and garnish with chopped scallions

SERVES 6

Sadly leeks are not common in our home kitchens. Some say they are too expensive. Some say they are too complicated to clean. Some say they'd rather use an onion. I say phooey to all that. They are beautiful alliums, the botanical family that includes onions and garlic. They should be treasured onions, though, not just ones that sit in the bottom of your pantry. Leeks exude a complex earthy sweetness that makes me melt. The aromas permeate but are not overpowering. Leeks are seductive.

This simple side dish uses a "sweets style" of cookery to develop a wonderful savory dish. The technique is identical to a dessert bread pudding.

* *

Preheat the oven to 400°F.

In a large bowl, place the bread, of the melted butter, and the thyme, tossing the bread to lightly coat in the butter. Spread the bread cubes out on a large rimmed baking sheet. Bake until golden and slightly crunchy, about 10 minutes. Return the cubes to the large bowl.

Reduce the oven temperature to 325°F.

Melt the 2 tablespoons of butter in a large skillet over medium-high heat. Add the leeks and sauté for 4 minutes. Add 2 tablespoons water and cover. At this point you are just encouraging some good steaming as opposed to browning. Reduce the heat to low and cook for 10 minutes. Remove from the stove and set aside.

Crack the egg into a large bowl and whisk in the heavy cream, milk, egg yolks, salt, pepper, and half of the Parmigiano. Mix this custard base into the leeks and then add the mixture to the bowl of bread cubes. Stir well to combine.

Butter a 10 by 8-inch baking dish or pie round and fill with the bread mixture. Sprinkle the remaining cheese over the bread mixture and bake in the oven for 20 to 25 minutes, until the custard has set and the top is golden.

SERVES 6

leek bread pudding

1-pound sourdough boule (crust on), cut into ½-inch cubes

4 tablespoons (½ stick) melted butter

1 teaspoon chopped fresh thyme leaves

2 tablespoons unsalted butter

6 medium leeks, white and light-green parts, cleaned (see Note page 242) and cut into ½-inch arcs

1 large egg

1 cup heavy whipping cream

1 cup whole milk

3 egg yolks from large eggs

1 teaspoon kosher salt

¼ teaspoon freshly ground black pepper

⅓ cup grated Parmigiano-Reggiano

NOTE: When cleaning leeks, lay them flat on a cutting board and slice them from the root end all the way up through the dark green. Gently rinse the two halves under cold water to get rid of the dirt that lies between layers of the leek. Think about how it grows and the dirt makes more sense... the white doesn't see the sun, and the layers grow on the outside, pushing up and grabbing dirt as they grow. As the leek peeks out of the ground it turns green from photosynthesis. The beautiful life of a leek! Then we eat it.

I tend to divide leeks into three areas. The dark greens get lopped off and are used in stock. The light green is good as a versatile cooking allium. The tender white is the top-grade part of the leek and should be used as such. In this recipe you can use the light green and white.

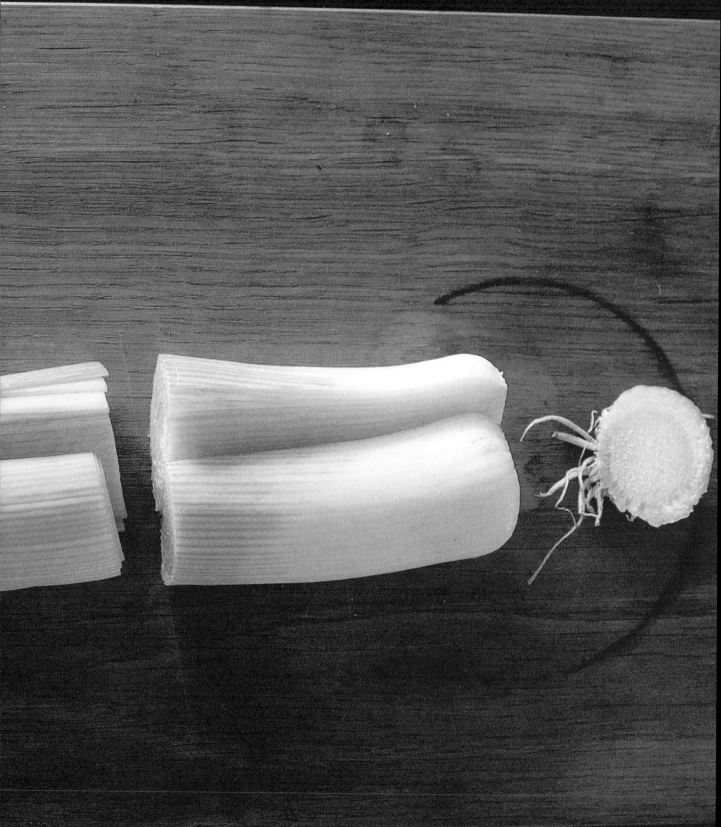

PiCKLES,
PuT-UPS
and
PANTRY ITEMS

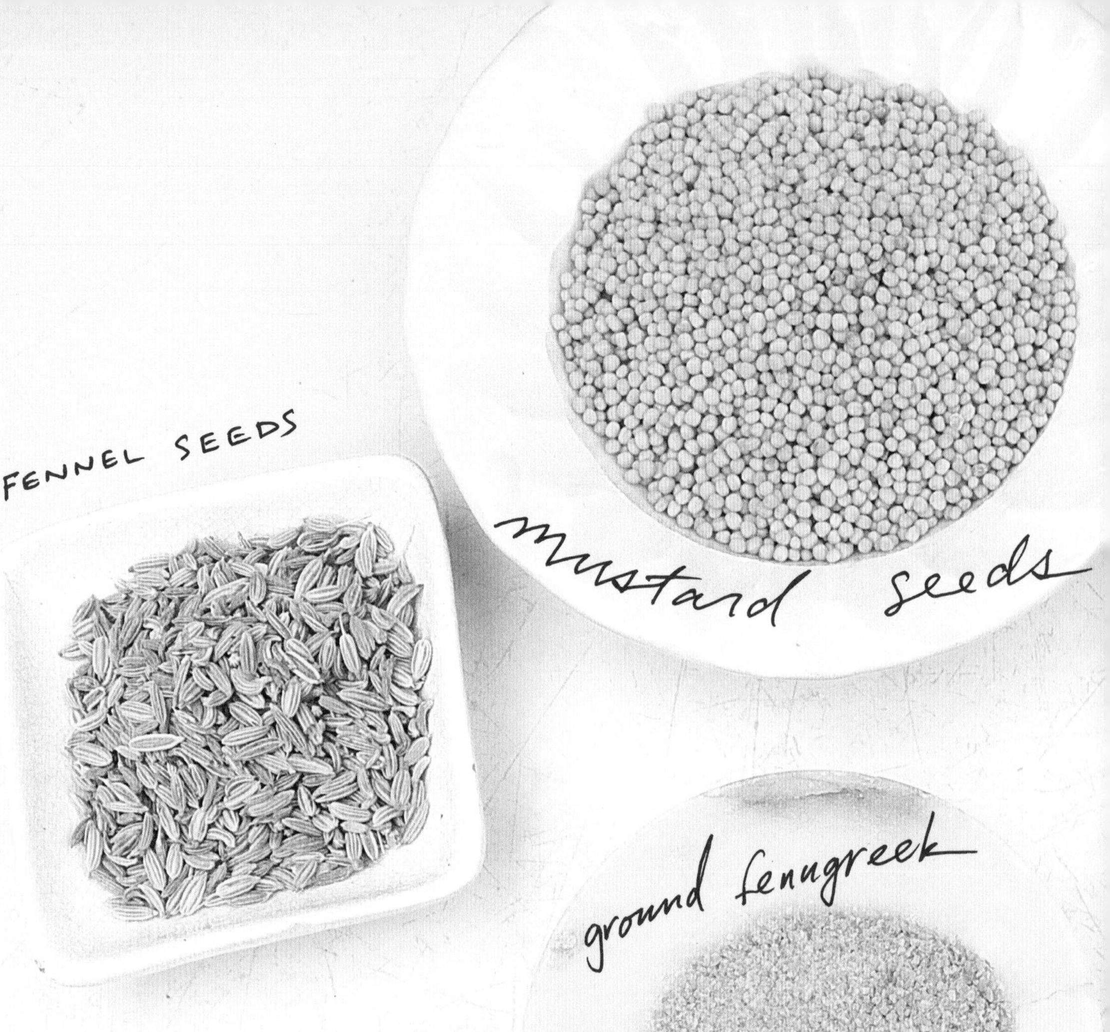

FENNEL SEEDS

mustard seeds

ground fenugreek

dark brown sugar

chile FLAKES

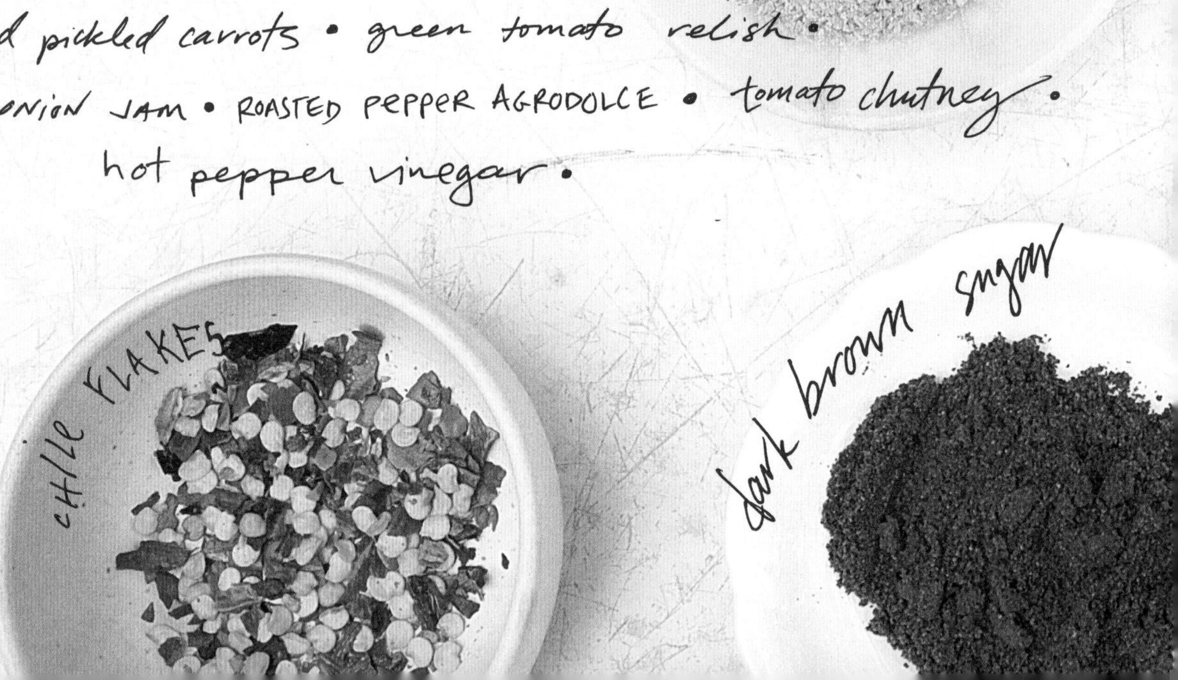

celery seeds

turmeric

When I opened up my Atlanta restaurant, Empire State South, in 2010, I took on a section of the menu new to most diners but familiar to Southern cooks: preserves. Not the sweet jams that are made everywhere and not the English or Indian chutneys, but rather the pickle-based cultural icons of the Southern table, such as chowchow, dilly pickles, pickled green tomatoes, spiced tomatoes, and packed-up okra. These little gems are the tableside items that we slather on our grilled pork; they blush our baked salmon and add nuance to our fried chicken.

The idea was that we would perform sommelier-like preserve service for the table, but that kind of got lost in the shuffle somewhere along the way. We still have the section, though, and it's still something that cheers my spirit because the preserves sell well, they just don't have that über fine-dining service that I'd hoped for. But then again, that's not me.

We love pickles because they parse out the seasonal bounty for us. They let the season stretch a bit longer so we can really savor the okra, beans, tomatoes, and peppers that make us smile. The items, upon preservation, fall into the realm of supporting role, but then again, so did Kevin Spacey in *The Usual Suspects.*

A wonderfully talented local woman named Liana Krissoff published a definitive book on modern canning called *Canning for a New Generation: Bold, Fresh Flavors for the Modern Pantry,* and it is a wonderfully insightful look into canning. The old Time-Life book series on canning is wonderful as well. Learning about these things will get you bonus points at the local farmer's market and points in your locavore club!

Bread 'n' Butter PICKLES

10 small pickling cucumbers
(4 to 5 inches long and 1½ inches
in diameter)

1 medium sweet onion, partial to
Vidalia when possible

¼ cup kosher salt

¼ cup fresh celery leaves

¼ teaspoon red pepper flakes

¼ teaspoon ground fenugreek

½ teaspoon fennel seeds

½ teaspoon ground turmeric

1 teaspoon mustard seeds

8 allspice berries

1½ cups cider vinegar

½ cup granulated sugar

½ cup sorghum or maple syrup

These pickles are what we pair with a torchon of foie gras, because of an unease with anything too fancy. This recipe is a very simple one to do and the results are just what you envision: tons more flavor than the store-boughts, a little less sweet and a little zestier. The better the cucumbers means the better the pickles, and local ones win most taste tests. Even better, grow your own! In a pinch the English-style cucumbers from Ontario are good because of their tender skin that hasn't been sprayed with that wax.

I don't like to cook the pickles in the pickling liquid, but rather to pour the liquid over the cucumbers and let the heat of the liquid do the rest. This means the vegetables don't overcook, resulting in a crisper pickle.

• •

Wash the cucumbers under cold water and then slice them into ⅓-inch-thick rounds. Peel the onion and slice into ⅓-inch strips. Mix the onion and cucumbers in a medium bowl and add half of the kosher salt. Toss well and let sit for 1 hour at room temperature.

Rinse the onion and cucumbers well using a colander and cold water to remove the salt. When thoroughly rinsed and drained, place them in a medium nonreactive bowl, tear the celery leaves into the mixture, and set aside. Pack the cucumbers, onion, and celery leaves into clean pint jars with the tops off.

Using a nonreactive pot, combine remaining salt, the red pepper flakes, fenugreek, fennel seeds, turmeric, mustard seeds, allspice, vinegar, sugar, sorghum, and ½ cup water. Bring to a rapid boil and then pour evenly over the cucumber mixture.

Attach the lids and leave them out on the counter for 2 hours and then place in the fridge. If you would like them to keep for the long haul, follow your jar manufacturer's directives for canning.

At this point the pickles are pretty much done but they will be at their best a day or two later. The shelf life, without hot canning processing, is about 10 days.

MAKES 3 TO 4 PINTS

PGTs are one of the backbones of Southern food. I am not sure who started the idea of green-tomato consumption, but evidently that person was not a resolute soul in watching tomatoes grow. Well, due to that impatience we do have a pretty wondrous array of things to do with green tomatoes, from frying to stewing to pickling.

I love these breaded and fried, chopped up on a big sandwich or burger, or minced into a simple salmon salad. Pickle on!

PICKLED GREEN TOMATOES

4 medium green tomatoes, no more than 3 inches in diameter

½ cup granulated raw sugar

½ teaspoon mustard seed

½ teaspoon fennel seed

¼ teaspoon hot smoked paprika

Pinch of red pepper flakes

⅔ cup cider vinegar

⅓ cup water

Wash and core the tomatoes. Using a sharp knife, cut the tomatoes in ¼-inch slices, like you were slicing the earth into pieces from South Pole to North Pole. Discard the top and bottom of each tomato and line them up how they were. It is as if you are putting the tomato puzzle back together.

Stack the tomatoes in two pint jars or one quart jar. I like the clean look of the pint jars because the tomatoes look so organized.

In a stainless-steel pot combine the sugar, mustard seed, fennel seed, paprika, red-pepper flakes, vinegar, and water. Bring to a boil and then simmer for 2 minutes. While the liquid is still hot, ladle it over the sliced tomatoes. Top with sterilized lids, tighten to finger tight, and process according to the jar manufacturer's instructions.

MAKES 3 PINTS

PICKLED OKRA

¾ pound small and unblemished okra

1 small red chile pepper, such as cayenne, red serrano, or Thai bird's-eye pepper

1 garlic clove

3 sprigs of fresh dill

1 teaspoon hot smoked paprika

1 teaspoon mustard seeds

1½ tablespoons kosher salt

1¼ cups cider vinegar

Okra has been sitting on the sidelines at the dance waiting for someone to become enamored of it for years. It smiles and winks and puts on a pretty good act but then it gets all gloppy. I think the word "gloppy" was invented with okra in mind. Okra is so much more than that. It is fresh and fun and crisp and lovely. It doesn't just have a role as a slimy texture component in sub-par gumbo. It wants to be loved.

That's where I come in. I am the block parent for unloved vegetables. Celery, okra, Brussels sprouts, and cardoons, they all come to me for safe harbor. I empower them by taking them away from the maligned recipes that give them their bad reputations. I find them recipes and culinary places where they belong, where they can be loved again.

Pickled okra is a classic where okra shines. It is a staple in our house for everything from a Bloody Mary to a condiment on a burger, or next to a pimiento cheese sandwich. This recipe multiplies well, so if you suddenly have a lot of okra and a nice afternoon, then by all means triple it up.

Pack the okra, chile pepper, garlic, and dill into a clean quart jar.

Combine the paprika, mustard seeds, salt, vinegar, and ¾ cup water in a medium-size stainless-steel pot and bring to a boil. Carefully ladle the hot pickling liquid into the jar, leaving ½ inch of headspace. Cap the jar and then process according to the manufacturer's instruction.

At this point the pickles are pretty much done but they will be at their best a day or two later. The shelf life, without hot canning processing, is about 10 days. With proper canning, it is 6 to 8 months.

MAKES 1 QUART

Cucumbers are very inexpensive and if you've ever had them in your garden you know why. They grow like weeds and produce a gazillion cukes per plant, so you had better get pickling if you have them planted.

This recipe is easily multiplied.

DILLY PICKLES

Pack the cucumbers, dill, and garlic into a clean quart jar. Combine the mustard seeds, peppercorns, dill seeds, salt, vinegar, and 2 cups water in a clean, medium stainless-steel pot and bring to a boil. Once the salt is completely dissolved, turn the heat off and ladle the pickling liquid into the jar to within ½ inch of the top. Adjust the lid and process according to the jar manufacturer's instructions.

At this point the pickles are pretty much done but they will be at their best a day or two later. The shelf life, without hot canning processing, is about 10 days. With proper canning, it is 6 to 8 months.

MAKES 1 QUART

1 pound pickling cucumbers, quartered into spears

5 sprigs of fresh dill

1 garlic clove, thinly sliced

1 teaspoon mustard seeds

4 black peppercorns

½ teaspoon dill seeds

2 tablespoons kosher salt

1 cup cider vinegar

Chowchow is a spicy, vinegary relish and a staple of the put-ups world. The core ingredients of cabbage, peppers, and green tomatoes seem to come up pretty fast at the same time of year and I am sure that this was a mixed condiment to make in bulk to deal with the vast harvest. You could add other things that are in abundance at your local market, or are growing out of control in your garden, such as pickling cucumbers or summer squash. Chowchow has a complex, almost Indian spice component to it and you could add some heat if you like things on the fiery side of the palate.

If you think that smaller jars would be better for your household, then just pack this into pint or half-pint jars. Ciao. Chowchow.

● ●

In a large bowl, mix together the cabbage, cauliflower, celery, tomatoes, bell peppers, sweet onion, scallions, and ginger. Add the salt, mix thoroughly, and let sit for about 2 hours at room temperature.

Drain the liquid that the salt has pulled out and place the vegetables in a large pot over medium-high heat. Add the vinegar, sugar, mustard seeds, dry mustard, celery seeds, cumin, turmeric, and chile powder. Bring to a boil and then simmer for 20 minutes.

Pack into jars and follow the manufacturer's directions for canning.

MAKES 2 QUARTS

CHOW CHOW

3 cups finely chopped green cabbage (see Note)

2 cups finely chopped cauliflower

1 cup peeled and minced celery

2 cups green tomatoes, cut into ½-inch dice

2 cups red bell peppers, cored, seeded, and chopped

1 cup minced sweet onion

1 cup minced scallions, white and green parts

2 tablespoons peeled and minced fresh ginger

2 tablespoons salt

2 cups cider vinegar

¾ cup granulated sugar

2 teaspoons yellow mustard seeds

1½ teaspoons dry mustard

1½ teaspoons celery seeds

1 teaspoon ground cumin

1 teaspoon ground turmeric

2 teaspoons chile powder

NOTE: when I say chopped, I mean pretty nicely chopped, not hacked into chunks. Hacking does not belong in the kitchen. Take time with a knife to make things pretty and precise. This attention to detail will make you proud of your work.

SPICY PICKLED TOMATOES

3 cups cherry tomatoes

1 teaspoon kosher salt

⅓ cup olive oil

3 shallots, minced

4 jalapeño chiles, sliced thinly

1 teaspoon cumin seeds, toasted and ground

1 teaspoon mustard seeds, toasted and ground to a paste

2 tablespoons freshly squeezed lime juice

2 tablespoons cane vinegar (page 135)

1 tablespoon light brown sugar

1 cup chopped fresh mint

1 cup chopped fresh flat-leaf parsley

This recipe is based on the wonderful fried-spice and chile condiments of India. Wonderfully full-flavored and voluptuous, it screams that we also love complex food!

Super 100s are a little cherry tomato variety that is kind of like candy. They are small and sweet and you start to eat them and just can't stop. Should you have three cups left over after intense snacking, this recipe would make a great pickled tomato condiment to go with everything from pastrami on rye to grilled chicken breasts. Continue!

Place the tomatoes in a medium glass or ceramic bowl that can withstand a little heat. Season the tomatoes with the kosher salt.

In a large fry pan bring the olive oil to a shimmer over medium-high heat, just below smoking point. Add the shallot and then the jalapeños. Fry off until tender, about 2 minutes, and then add the cumin and the mustard-seed paste. Toast for about 1 minute and remove from the heat.

Let cool slightly and carefully add the lime juice, vinegar, and brown sugar and then pour this mixture over the seasoned tomatoes. Add the mint and parsley and let sit at room temperature for about 2 hours for the flavors to mature.

You can just store this one in the fridge and use it for up to 2 weeks. If you canned it, it would keep for 6 to 8 months.

MAKES 2 QUARTS

Carrots are my go-to snack. I eat about a pound a day around the kitchen, raw and crunchy. I don't know that my eyesight is any better, but who knows. This pickled version is great on a pickle plate or chopped up on a pork sandwich.

GINGERED PICKLED CARROTS

Peel the carrots and cut them into batons about 4 inches long by ½-inch thick. Toss with the ginger and pack into clean, sterilized jars.

Combine 1 cup water with the vinegar, turbinado sugar, and salt in a saucepan and bring to a boil. Pour the mixture over the carrots, leaving about ½ inch of space at the top of each jar.

At this point the pickles are pretty much done but they will be at their best a day or two later. The shelf life, without hot canning processing, is about 10 days. With proper canning, it is 6 to 8 months.

MAKES 3 PINTS

1 pound smaller organic carrots
3 tablespoons matchsticks of peeled fresh ginger
1 cup vinegar
¼ cup turbinado sugar
1 tablespoon kosher salt

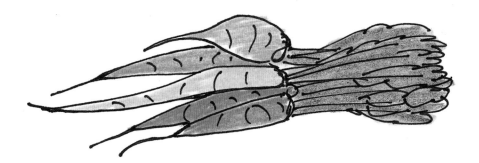

GREEN toMATO RELiSH

1 tablespoon olive oil

¼ cup minced scallions, white parts only

1 garlic clove, minced

1 minced jalapeño chile, seeds and all

3 medium-size green tomatoes, chopped

½ teaspoon kosher salt

½ cup sherry vinegar

⅓ cup granulated sugar

½ teaspoon dry mustard

½ teaspoon hot smoked paprika

1 teaspoon ground turmeric

¼ teaspoon ground coriander

½ teaspoon red pepper flakes

½ teaspoon freshly ground black pepper

This is a bright and simple chutney meant to adorn anything from a hot dog to a pork chop. It would be great with country ham on a biscuit or as a finishing touch to a nice piece of fried catfish.

• •

Heat the olive oil over medium heat in a saucepan. Add the scallions, garlic, and jalapeños and sauté until the scallions are translucent. Add the tomatoes and salt. Cook for 10 minutes over medium heat. Add the vinegar, sugar, mustard, paprika, turmeric, coriander, red pepper flakes, and black pepper and cook for 10 more minutes. Spoon the hot chutney into a quart jar and process according to the jar manufacturer's instructions.

The shelf life, without hot canning processing, is about 10 days. With proper canning, it is 6 to 8 months.

MAKES 1 QUART

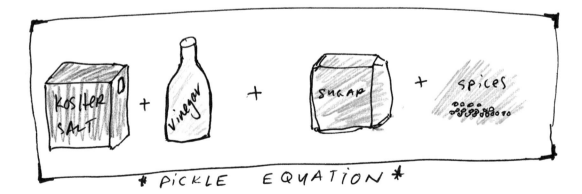

* PiCKLE EQUATION *

When I think of sweet onions I think about beautiful early summer Vidalias from Vidalia, Georgia. They are smaller and less cured than what is normally carried at your local food store. Most onions are harvested and then cured, or laid out to develop an outer skin. This allows them to be kept in your pantry through the year, until the new harvest arrives. Spring onions do not go through this curing process.

Spring Vidalias are about the size of a squash ball with beautiful greens on top and a lovely spiciness in the front palate that moves into a sweet flavor at the back of the tongue. Nowadays there are many options in your local store when it comes to sweet spring onions; I am just geographically inclined toward Vidalia. From Texas to Hawaii, from Virginia to Florida, there is a good local sweet onion somewhere near you . . . Now, go and find it.

This is a classic condiment to have for any occasion. In the summer it's on my burger, in the winter it's on my turkey sandwiches, and in fancier circumstances it appears alongside the torchon de foie gras with peppered mango and toasted brioche.

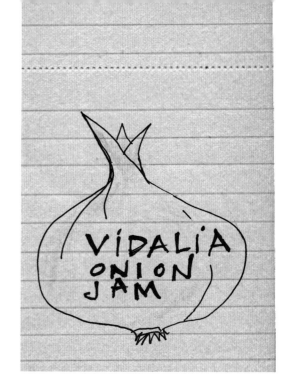

¼ pound (1 stick) unsalted butter
4 cups thinly sliced sweet onions
1 tablespoon soy sauce
1 tablespoon balsamic vinegar
1 teaspoon dark brown sugar
1 teaspoon chopped fresh thyme leaves (no stems)
¼ teaspoon kosher salt
¼ teaspoon freshly ground black pepper

In a large pot over medium heat, melt the butter. When the butter begins to bubble and froth, add the onions and cook down for 15 minutes, until the onions are well colored and limp.

Add the soy, balsamic, brown sugar, and thyme. Cook for 15 minutes and then add ½ cup water. Cook for 10 more minutes and then add another ½ cup water. Cook for 5 minutes and then remove from the heat and season with the salt and pepper. The jam is done cooking at this point. Pour the jam into a bowl to get it away from the heat of the pot and then place that bowl in a bath of ice water. What you're trying to do is bring the jam back into the safety zone of temperatures, quickly and cleanly. Cool and transfer to a clean, sealable container. The jam will keep in the refrigerator for up to 2 weeks.

MAKES 2 CUPS

ROASTED pepper AGRODOLCE

2 yellow bell peppers

2 red bell peppers

2 tablespoons raisins

¼ cup Madeira

2 tablespoons extra-virgin olive oil

2 tablespoons balsamic vinegar (see page 263)

2 garlic cloves, thinly sliced

2 tablespoons chopped fresh flat-leaf parsley

½ teaspoon kosher salt

Agrodolce means "sour-sweet." I find we are always looking for balance in our food. The sweet comes from the peppers and the sour comes from the vinegar.

To roast the peppers, here are some choices:

1. Place the naked peppers, one at a time, on a gas burner to char.

2. Preheat the oven to 450°F. Lightly rub the peppers with olive oil, place on a rimmed sheet pan, and roast for 15 minutes, turning them halfway through, or until charred on all sides.

3. Lightly rub the peppers with olive oil and grill them on a charcoal or gas outdoor grill until uniformly charred.

In all three instances you want to get them nicely charred and then place them in a medium bowl, cover with plastic wrap, and have the skins loosen up for 10 minutes. Then remove the plastic and gently rinse the peppers under cold water to get rid of all the charred skin. Cut the peppers in half and discard the seeds and stem. Cut the roasted peppers into 1 by 1-inch chunks and place in the medium bowl.

Combine the raisins and Madeira in a small pot on low heat and cook for 5 minutes to plump the raisins. Meanwhile add the olive oil, balsamic, garlic, parsley, and salt to the peppers. Stir well. Once the raisins have plumped out, add them with the remaining Madeira to the peppers.

Pack the agrodolce into a quart jar or two pint jars. It will keep for about 10 days in the fridge.

MAKES 2 CUPS

BALSAMIC VINEGAR
Let's chat about balsamic vinegar for a moment:

Buy good stuff. Not the stuff that costs a hundred dollars for a tiny bottle, but stuff that is not just brown vinegar. The really spendy stuff is *Aceto Balsamico Tradizionale* and the key word in that phrase is "Tradizionale," which the inexpensive copycats are legally prohibited from using. There are some good simple "Condimento" grade vinegars that are fine and reasonable. Traditional-method balsamic is aged Trebbiano grape juice stored in a series of wooden barrels. These barrels impart flavors and color to the juice over the twelve, eighteen, or even twenty-five years it spends in the barrel. What we are looking for is a vinegar made by some of the prized Tradizionale producers that has only been aged six or eight years and is thus less expensive. The cheap balsamics (notice I did not say inexpensive) are colored white vinegars with artificial flavors. Avoid these by reading the ingredient list.

TOMATO CHUTNEY

½ teaspoon fenugreek seeds

½ teaspoon cumin seeds

½ teaspoon yellow mustard seeds

⅓ cup extra-virgin olive oil

1 large yellow onion, minced

1 tablespoon minced fresh garlic
   (always use fresh garlic, not the
   pre-minced stuff!)

2 tablespoons minced and peeled
   ginger

2 jalapeño chiles, cored, seeded, and
   minced

12 roma tomatoes, coarsely chopped

½ teaspoon kosher salt

½ cup chopped fresh cilantro

¼ cup chopped fresh flat-leaf parsley

This will make more than you'll need but it will stay fresh for about a week and is awesome on a roast beef sandwich or as a nice accompaniment to a great cheddar.

In a small cast-iron skillet, toast the fenugreek, cumin, and mustard seeds for 30 seconds over medium heat. Remove from the heat and lightly grind in a clean spice grinder.

   Warm the olive oil in a large shallow pot (rondeau) over medium-high heat. Add the onion, cook for 2 minutes, and then raise the heat to high. Add the garlic, ginger, and jalapeños and sauté for 3 minutes.

   Add the spices, tomatoes, and salt and cook for about 5 minutes on high heat, or until the tomatoes look like a sizzled, lightly cooked, but thick tomato sauce. Reduce the heat to medium and cook for 30 minutes, stirring every minute or so. Remove from the heat and add the cilantro and parsley.

MAKES 5 CUPS

Pepper vinegar sits in our fridge, on the farm table in the dining room, in the cupboard, and beside the stove. It gets sloshed onto collards and finished peas, and it gets shaken over rice and beans. With a little olive oil it's the simplest salad dressing ever. As for the type of pepper to use, that's up to you. Tabasco, cayenne, Thai bird's-eye, or even a calmer serrano will provide more than enough kick for my palate.

1 cup hot peppers, such as Tabasco, cayenne, Thai bird's-eye, or serrano

3 cups cider vinegar

Slit the peppers. This makes for a more intense flavor. Place the peppers in a quart Mason jar and then cover with the room temperature vinegar. Cap and let sit in a cool dark place for 2 to 3 weeks.

Once the flavors have matured, strain and transfer the vinegar to a wine bottle and cap it with a bar pour spout for ease of use.

MAKES 1 QUART

WHIPPED CREAM
and other delights

Dessert plays a major role in the South. From pies to layer cakes to banana pudding, dessert is a serious topic around here. For a chef with only a mild sweet tooth, I have always chosen a pretty neutral stance on new interpretations of Southern classics. If it ain't broke don't fix it. What I do have is a long list of Southern dessert mentors like Karen Barker, Angie Mosier, Phoebe Lawless, and our own Shae Rehmel to set me straight and give me hints, tidbits, and sweet inspirations.

Desserts are the final offering of a dinner, apart from that last nip of bourbon that we're fond of around here. In the summer at my family's cottage in Canada, there is always a pie in the oven, a cobbler cooling on the stove, or maple tarts sitting on the windowsill. At home in Athens I find myself making things the kids will love, like chess pie and apple brown betty. Having dessert for us means making time to finish out a meal right, to spend time over coffee or bourbon with the ones we love, whether at home, at the cottage, or at one of my restaurants.

Making great desserts is easier said than done. It takes precision and careful reading of the recipe to make it all turn out right. It also takes a keen eye for the ripeness of fruit and the proper kneading of doughs. Do remember that those who make great desserts are loved that much more.

Pie Chest. Chess Pie. The pie that sat in the chest cooling.

This is a straightforward, classic pie of the South. In Tennessee they make two or three and pile them on top of each other for Stacked Chess Pie! This is my go-to dessert for all occasions. If blackberries aren't in season you can make a fruit compote out of whatever is, from peaches to strawberries to figs to apples. Serve this with Vanilla Bean Ice Cream (page 296).

You will need eight 4-inch tartlet molds (available at good kitchenware stores).

● ●

Preheat the oven to 375°F.

Roll the dough out to ¼ inch thick and cut eight 6-inch rounds for the 4-inch tartlet molds. Fill the molds with dough, cut off excess dough from the sides, and refrigerate for 15 minutes.

Cut pieces of aluminum foil to cover each tartlet mold and delicately press them into the molds. Fill with pie weights or dried beans and place on a rimmed baking sheet on the middle rack in the oven. Bake for 10 minutes. Take out the tartlets, remove the pie weights and the foil, and bake for another 8 to 10 minutes, or until the edges are golden and the bottom of the crust is dry.

Reduce the oven temperature to 330°F.

In a food processor, grind the sugar with the lemon zest.

In a large bowl, beat the butter and salt with the sugar and lemon zest mixture until well blended. Add the eggs and corn syrup, then add the milk. Add the cornmeal and flour. Add the lemon juice.

Fill the cooled prebaked shells with the lemon filling, place them back on the baking sheet, and bake for 10 minutes. Rotate the pies and continue baking for 10 minutes. Bake for another 5 to 10 minutes, checking every couple of minutes, until the filling is set and the top is slightly golden. Remove from the oven. Allow to cool slightly.

Serve warm with 2 tablespoons of blackberry compote.

MAKES 8 SMALL PIES

LEMON CHESS PIES with blackberry compote

½ recipe Pie Dough crust (recipe follows)

1¾ cups granulated sugar

3 tablespoons grated lemon zest

½ cup (1 stick) unsalted butter, softened

Pinch of salt

5 eggs

¼ cup corn syrup

1 cup whole milk

1 tablespoon cornmeal

2 tablespoons all-purpose flour

¼ cup freshly squeezed lemon juice

8 tablespoons cooled Blackberry Compote (see page 272)

recipe continues ⟶

PIE DOUGH

**MAKES ENOUGH FOR TWO 9-INCH
ROUND PIES**

I like to make the dough a day ahead so I don't have to wait
for it to rest when I'm ready to make pie.

5¾ cups all-purpose flour
2 teaspoons kosher salt

1 pound (4 sticks) cold
   unsalted butter, cubed
½ cup cold water

Mix the flour and salt together in a large mixing bowl. Put the
mixture into a food processor and place the butter on top. Mix
until the butter is pea-size and the mixture has a cornmeal
consistency.

In a small bowl, combine the cold water with several ice
cubes. Let the ice cubes melt a little to allow the water to
become very cold. Measure out ½ cup plus 1 tablespoon of
the water.

Add the ice-cold water to the food processor while on and
process until the dough just comes together. Turn off the
processor and empty the dough into a large bowl.

Give the dough a couple of kneads to bring it together.
Divide the dough evenly into two separate pieces, wrap in
plastic, and flatten to make rolling out easier later.

Let the dough rest in the fridge for at least 30 minutes.
This pie dough can sit in the fridge for 3 days or in the freezer
for up to 2 weeks.

BLACKBERRY COMPOTE

MAKES 2 CUPS

¼ cup granulated sugar
2 tablespoons dessert wine,
   such as a Muscat or Vin
   Santo

Pinch of salt
Pinch of ground cinnamon
1½ cups blackberries

In a small saucepan, bring the sugar, wine, salt, and cinnamon
to a simmer and allow to simmer for 2 minutes. Add the
blackberries and cook while stirring for 1 minute. Turn off the
heat and pour the compote into a clean bowl and chill.

Former Five and Ten pastry chef Lynda Oosterhuis is the mastermind behind this dessert. Somewhere around 2001 Lynda called me to inquire about a position in the pastry department. For some reason, still not really clear to me, Lynda was in Athens, having just left the employ of Bouley Bakery in New York City. They had just received a great review and here was a vastly overqualified person offering to revamp the bread and pastry area at my little Five and Ten. Obviously I accepted. Lynda stayed on for about two years and she was, and still is, an awe-inspiring person responsible for much of the greatness that Five and Ten achieved. This is a great and easy recipe that will become a staple for your sweets kitchen. Serve with cinnamon ice cream (see page 297).

You will need eight 4-ounce ramekins.

1 teaspoon unsalted butter, plus
  5 tablespoons unsalted butter,
  melted
2 teaspoons granulated sugar
22 medjool dates (about 1½ cups),
  pitted and chopped
1 cup plus 2 tablespoons whole milk
Grated zest of 2 oranges
½ vanilla bean, scraped, seeds only
1 cup all-purpose flour
2 teaspoons baking powder
½ cup packed light brown sugar
1 teaspoon ground cinnamon
1 teaspoon freshly grated nutmeg
1 teaspoon salt
2 eggs
5 tablespoons unsalted butter, melted
2 cups bread crumbs, from fresh
  sandwich bread, roughly torn

Preheat the oven to 325°F.

Using the 1 teaspoon of butter, lightly grease the eight 4-ounce ramekins. Sprinkle each ramekin with a pinch of granulated sugar and set aside.

Combine the dates and milk in a small saucepan and cook over low heat for 10 minutes. Add the orange zest and vanilla seeds to the date and milk mixture.

In a medium mixing bowl, combine the flour, baking powder, brown sugar, cinnamon, nutmeg, and salt.

In a large mixing bowl fitted with the paddle attachment, beat the eggs until fluffy, about 5 minutes. Add the remaining butter, the bread crumbs, and the date mixture, beating until just combined. Slowly mix in the dry ingredients in two stages, finishing off with a spatula.

Evenly distribute the pudding mixture into the buttered and sugared ramekins.

Fill up a kettle with water and bring to a boil.

Place the ramekins in a baking dish with sides (such as a roasting pan or large casserole dish). Place the pan on the oven rack. Carefully pour the hot water from the kettle into the baking dish until it comes halfway up the ramekins.

Bake for 45 minutes to 1 hour, until the puddings have souffléd and are just firm to the touch.

SERVES 8

Really Good Peach Pie

2 Pie Dough crusts (page 272)

½ cup packed light brown sugar

⅓ cup plus 1 tablespoon granulated sugar

3 tablespoons arrowroot

2 teaspoons ground cinnamon

Pinch of salt

8 large peaches (peeled, pitted, and sliced into ½-inch thick slices)

1½ tablespoons cold unsalted butter, cut into small cubes

1 egg (for egg wash)

♥ YOUR PEACHES

The sweet South is about pies and cakes. The best pies last about five minutes on the table. Molten chocolate cake has nothing on a peach pie. I have been very lucky in life to have eaten great desserts from some of the awesome pastry chefs of the South, such as Phoebe Lawless, Karen Barker, Kathryn King, Angie Mosier, and our own Shae Rehmel, who offers up this recipe. Serve with Vanilla Bean Ice Cream (page 296).

Preheat the oven to 415°F.

Flour the surface of a cutting board and place one piece of the pie dough on top of the flour. Roll the dough out to ¼ inch thick. Place the dough into a 9-inch pie pan and trim the edges so that there is about 1 inch hanging over the side.

Roll out the second piece of pie dough and punch out a design with a small cookie cutter, reserving the punched-out dough. Set the crust aside.

Mix the brown sugar, ⅓ cup of the granulated sugar, the arrowroot, cinnamon, and salt together in a large bowl. Add the peaches to the sugar and spice mix. Once combined, immediately place into the pie crust. If the mixture sits too long in the bowl it gets juicy and difficult to work with.

Sprinkle the small butter cubes on the top of the fruit. Place the second crust over the filling and seal the edges of the two crusts. Trim any excess dough with scissors and crimp the edges decoratively. Place the small punch-outs of pie dough on top.

Crack the egg into a small bowl and beat well. Using a soft pastry brush, brush the top of the pie and crust with the egg and then sprinkle with the remaining tablespoon of sugar.

Place the pie in the freezer for 15 minutes.

Place a baking sheet in the oven and allow it to get nice and hot.

Remove the pie from the freezer and place it on the hot baking sheet in the oven. Bake at 415°F for 15 minutes. Reduce the temperature to 370°F and continue baking for 30 minutes, or until the pie is golden brown and bubbling.

Cool and serve with vanilla ice cream.

MAKES ONE 9-INCH PIE; SERVES 8

This has been a staple of mine for years and I never tire of it. I love the baked pears and the pecans together. Pecans litter the ground around here for about two months from September until November and my kids have always been pretty savvy to find a rock and crack them open. I remember Beatrice doing that when she was two years old outside her daycare. That makes a lot of sense when you realize the word "pecan" derives from an Algonquin term for "nut you open with rock."

I use a melon baller to scoop out the seed area of the apples and pears. Tricks of the trade.

This would rock with some homemade sorghum ice cream (see page 297).

Preheat the oven to 350°F.

Melt the butter in a 9-inch cast-iron skillet over medium heat. Add the pears and orange zest and cook for 2 to 3 minutes, stirring occasionally. Add the orange juice, ginger, vanilla seeds, and sugar and cook for another 5 to 7 minutes, until the pears are tender but still have a bite. Remove the pears from the liquid with a slotted spoon and set aside.

Increase the heat to medium high and continue to cook the liquid until it's thickened to a caramel-like state, 4 to 5 minutes. Turn off the heat. Allow the liquid to cool for a few minutes.

Arrange the pears in a desired design on top of the reduced sugar mixture. Sprinkle with the chopped pecans.

Spread the cake batter over the top of the pears. Bake for 30 to 35 minutes, until the cake springs back just slightly when touched. Allow to cool for 5 minutes.

Run a knife around the edge of the cake and unmold by carefully flipping the skillet onto a large serving plate. Serve warm with homemade sorghum ice cream.

MAKES ONE 9-INCH CAKE; SERVES 8 TO 12

PEAR & PECAN flip cake

4 tablespoons (½ stick) butter

4 pears, peeled, scooped of seeds, and cut into ¼-inch slices

Zest and juice of 1 orange

1 teaspoon grated fresh peeled ginger

½ vanilla bean, scraped seeds only

1 cup granulated sugar

¾ cup pecans, toasted and coarsely chopped

Cake Batter (recipe follows)

recipe continues ⟶

CAKE BATTER

½ cup (1 stick) unsalted butter, softened
½ cup packed light brown sugar
½ cup granulated sugar
½ vanilla bean, scraped seeds only
1 teaspoon ground cinnamon
3 eggs, at room temperature
2 tablespoons buttermilk
1¼ cups all-purpose flour
¼ cup cornmeal
1¾ teaspoons baking powder
½ teaspoon salt

In a large mixing bowl, cream the butter, brown sugar, granulated sugar, vanilla seeds, and cinnamon with an electric mixer until pale and fluffy.

Crack the eggs into a medium bowl, add the buttermilk, and whisk to combine. Slowly add the egg mixture to the butter mixture, stirring gently to combine.

In a medium bowl, combine the flour, cornmeal, baking powder, and salt. Add the dry mixture to the wet all at once, turn on the mixer, and mix for about 30 seconds.

This batter can also be baked on its own and served with a fruit compote, homemade ice cream, or used in a pineapple upside-down cake.

TEA CRÈME BRÛLÉE

Sweet tea anything! I once had to do a cooking-with-tea demonstration and this is what I came up with. This brûlée is unique, tastes great, and is an instructive beginning to the world of custards. Serve with your favorite cookie. Something with a crunchy texture is nice because it will contrast with the smooth and cool custard.

I like to make the base one day ahead of time and bake the brûlées a day before I want to serve them. They can be made all in the same day but it is much easier to split up the work over a couple of days.

You will need six ramekins.

3½ cups heavy cream

1 cup granulated sugar

2 tea bags, or 2 tablespoons loose-leaf tea (I like to use Earl Grey)

7 egg yolks

Preheat the oven to 325°F (300°F if you are using a convection oven).

In a medium saucepan, heat the cream and ¼ cup of the granulated sugar on medium-high heat until steaming, 5 to 8 minutes.

Add the tea bags or loose tea of your choice and steep for 3 minutes. If using herbal tea you can steep for longer to infuse with flavor; black tea leaves will impart too much tannin if steeped for too long. Remove tea bags.

In a small bowl, whisk together another ¼ cup of the granulated sugar and the egg yolks until pale in color. Temper the hot cream mixture into the sugar and egg yolks by adding just a tablespoon at a time of the hot cream while whisking. As long as you work slowly the egg yolks won't scramble. When at least half of the hot cream has been slowly added to the yolks, pour the remaining hot cream into the yolks and stir until all of the sugar is dissolved.

Strain this base into a medium heat-proof glass bowl, cover, and chill in an ice bath. Refrigerate if you are not baking the brûlées right away. Otherwise, skim off any excess foam created from whisking and pour evenly into 6 individual ramekins.

Place the ramekins in a baking dish that is at least 2 inches deep. Slowly pour warm water into the baking dish until it comes halfway up the ramekins. Cover the dish with aluminum foil and crimp the edges to keep the moisture in. Bake for 50 minutes.

Pull the pan slightly out of the oven, remove a corner of the aluminum foil, and carefully jiggle one ramekin. You want the custard to have set to a relative solid. When you jiggle it, the custard should shake for 1 second and then stop. If it continues to shake then it needs more oven time. If it's not done, replace the foil, rotate the pan, and continue baking for 8 minutes, then check again and give it more time if needed until fully set. This dessert can be a little tricky if it's your first time baking a custard, so be patient. You'll understand the process even better the next time you make it.

When done, remove the tray and make sure the custards are all set. Pull off the aluminum foil. Remove the ramekins from the water bath using tongs and place the ramekins in the refrigerator for at least 3 hours.

Evenly sprinkle about a tablespoon of the remaining sugar on top of each cold custard and gently brown the sugar with a kitchen blowtorch. If you don't have a torch, set your oven to broil and place the rack as close to the top as possible. When the oven is fully heated, sprinkle the tops with sugar and place directly in the oven. Watch closely so you don't overcook. Remove when the sugar is fully melted and dark brown, 2 to 3 minutes. Serve warm.

SERVES 6

I have a friend who is a superstar in the chef world. Suffice it to say he wears orange clogs. You know who I mean. Mario is brilliant. Way back years ago I staged—restaurant lingo for doing an externship—at his restaurants in Manhattan. It was a wonderful opportunity. One thing that stuck with me was a pork they were doing at one of the kitchens with whole clusters of roasted grapes. It looked beautiful, but, more important, I loved the roasted concentrated flavor in the grapes. Since then we have been serving cheese with roasted grapes at the restaurant and I have been making this wonderful clafouti with them as well. A clafouti is a very classic French dessert that is fruit encased in a thick batter. It looks and tastes like a thick pancake but that doesn't really do it justice. It is great. Think pancake made by Joël Robuchon, not IHOP. Serve with peanut ice cream (see page 297) and candied peanuts (see page 298).

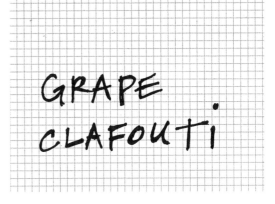

GRAPE CLAFOUTI

3 cups red grapes, washed, stems removed

6 eggs

¾ cup whole milk

¾ cup crème fraîche or heavy cream

½ cup granulated sugar

1 vanilla bean, scraped seeds only

1 teaspoon pure vanilla extract

Pinch of salt

½ cup all-purpose flour

2 teaspoons tawny port

Preheat the oven to 400°F.

Grease a 9-inch pie pan and fill it with the grapes. Roast in the oven for 10 to 15 minutes until the skins start to pop and release some of the juice.

While the grapes are roasting, in a blender process the eggs, milk, crème fraîche, sugar, vanilla seeds, vanilla extract, and salt until smooth. Add the flour and pulse until well combined. Pass the batter through a sieve and let it rest at room temperature for 30 minutes.

Remove the grapes from the baking dish and let rest for a few minutes to cool off. Douse the grapes with the port. Then place them back in the baking dish and pour the batter over the grapes. Place the baking dish in the oven and bake for 20 minutes, or until the batter is set.

Serve warm with peanut ice cream and candied peanuts.

SERVES 8 TO 10

Apple Brown Betty with Sorghum Zabaglione

6 to 8 apples (Gala or Granny Smith), peeled, cored, and cut into ¼-inch slices

½ cup granulated sugar

2 teaspoons ground cinnamon

½ teaspoon ground ginger

Juice of 1 lemon

½ vanilla bean, seeds and pod

½ loaf bread, crust removed (any type of white bread is fine)

6 tablespoons (¾ stick) unsalted butter

2 tablespoons packed light brown sugar

3 cups Sorghum Zabaglione (recipe follows)

I love apples. I have this recurring dream where I leave the stress of the restaurant world behind and start a cider house, making exquisite hard cider. I start at sunrise and I finish in the mid-afternoon and retire to the farmhouse to cook a dinner for Mary and the girls.

Apple brown betty is like a crisp made with bread crumbs. It's a wonderful dessert that is so simple and so rewarding in results. This is a good one for roping the kids into helping. Those apples aren't going to peel themselves.

Zabaglione is also known in France as sabayon. It is a custard-based dessert, cooked with a dessert wine. I stabilize mine with whipped cream and serve it cold, whereas in Italy and France you often see them served warm. Kind of like an eggnog in heaven.

Preheat the oven to 350°F. Lightly butter an 8 by 8-inch baking dish.

In a large bowl, toss the apples with the granulated sugar, cinnamon, ginger, lemon juice, and the vanilla pod and seeds. Cover with plastic wrap and let sit for 30 minutes.

Tear the bread up and pulse in a food processor. Spread out the bread crumbs on a rimmed baking sheet and toast in the oven for 5 to 8 minutes, until golden. Set aside.

While the bread crumbs are toasting, place 4 tablespoons of the butter into a small saucepan over medium heat. Cook until the milk solids separate from the fat and the butter begins to brown.

In a medium bowl, mix the bread crumbs, brown sugar, and warm brown butter together. Add about one-quarter of the bread-crumb mixture to the apples. Toss to combine.

Fill the prepared baking dish with the apple mixture. Dot with the remaining 2 tablespoons of butter.

Cover the top with the remaining bread-crumb mixture. Press down firmly all over the top so that the mixture is tightly packed in the dish.

Bake on the middle rack of the oven until the apples are soft and the juices start to bubble, 25 to 35 minutes.

Serve warm and with a ½-cup scoop of sorghum zabaglione on top of each portion.

SERVES 6

SORGHUM ZABAGLIONE

SERVES 6 OR MAKES 3 CUPS

1 cup heavy cream
3 egg yolks
¼ cup sorghum
¼ teaspoon grated lemon zest
1 tablespoon freshly squeezed lemon juice
1 vanilla bean, scraped seeds only
¾ cup Riesling

Put the heavy cream in a mixing bowl and whip it by hand with a balloon whisk until you have softly whipped cream. Most people overwhip cream, so make sure you have very silky smooth soft peaks and not firm cream with an almost broken texture. Place the whipped cream in the fridge.

In a large stainless-steel or heat-proof glass bowl, whisk the egg yolks with the sorghum, lemon zest, lemon juice, vanilla seeds, and Riesling until well mixed, about 2 minutes.

Create a double boiler by placing a large pot on the stove over medium-high heat with 2 inches of water in it. Insert the bowl of egg yolks into the pot and whisk vigorously. The heat is there but the water is insulating the eggs from scrambling. Whisk for about 5 minutes, making sure not to get the eggs too hot. If you feel like they are in jeopardy of scrambling, remove the bowl from the heat and then return it to the pot when it has stabilized. You should have very nice ribbon custard at this point, almost double in volume what you started with.

Remove the bowl from the heat and continue whisking until the zabaglione base is thick and has cooled to room temperature.

Fold the zabaglione base into the whipped cream and set aside. The zabaglione can sit in the fridge up to 24 hours before it deflates.

APPLES to APPLES

Let's think about an apple in February. The apple is picked in Chile by a migrant picker.

It goes onto a truck and then into a sorter. The apple gets graded, cleaned, waxed, and stickered. It gets packed into a box and then sits for a day or two. It goes onto another truck and is off to customs. It clears customs and then gets onto a very big boat. It floats on the water for a week. It arrives in New York and goes to a warehouse. A broker buys the fruit and then moves it, via truck, to another warehouse. A produce wholesaler buys a bunch of it and ships it down to the commercial vegetable market near the airport in Atlanta. A local company buys the product there and trucks it to a grocer. The grocer packs the apples into a cooler and after some time the apples get onto the shelf. The apples, shiny and waxy, cost $1.99 per pound.

Let me tell you how I like to order apples. First of all, the key is to order apples in season. Apple season in Georgia is from August to November. So, say in September, a fax comes to me on Tuesdays from a small cooperative of farms called the Northeast Farmers of Georgia. It is sent by a dear man named Bill. I put a check next to a box for Arkansas Blacks, a wonderful Southern crisp heirloom apple. Bill gets the fax and calls the farmer. The farmer picks the apples and delivers them to Bill, and Bill drives them to me in Athens. It is so simple.

This process supports Bill. It supports the farmer. It supports my local economy. It lessens the consumption cost. It lowers the amount of non-renewable resources used to ship the items to me. It reduces the number of hands that touch my product. Oh, and the apples taste better—much better.

There is a fig tree in the yard of our former house. It has been a very fruitful tree, so every year I have to make some jams and tarts and a number of savory fig recipes just to keep up with the fruit production. This is a recipe inspired by my short tenure at a very highfalutin restaurant in San Francisco where they made an awesome fig tart paired with a black licorice ice cream.

You will need six 4-inch tartlet molds.

Preheat the oven to 350°F.

Roll out the tart dough and fill six 4-inch tartlet molds. Place the dough-filled molds in the fridge for 20 minutes.

Line the shells with aluminum foil and fill with pie weights or dried beans.

Place the shells on a rimmed baking sheet and bake on the middle rack for 10 minutes, or until the outer crust is medium brown and the bottoms are completely dried out.

Remove the shells from the oven and allow to cool. Remove the weights and foil and pop the shells out of the molds.

Grease a baking dish with 1 tablespoon of the butter and fill the dish with the figs. Pour the orange juice, the 2 tablespoons of honey, and the sugar on top and dot the figs with the remaining tablespoon of butter. Cover the baking dish with foil and roast in the oven for 10 to 15 minutes, until the figs are softened but still have structure.

Remove the figs from the baking dish and set aside.

Fill the tart shells with a thin layer of apricot preserves. Fill with the whipped cream to no higher than the top of the shell. Arrange the fig slices in a decorative manner on top of the whipped cream. Drizzle each tart with 1 teaspoon of honey and ½ tablespoon of candied nuts.

MAKES 6 SMALL TARTS

Tart Dough (recipe follows)
2 tablespoons unsalted butter
12 fresh figs, quartered
Juice of 1 orange
2 tablespoons plus 6 teaspoons honey
1 tablespoon granulated sugar
6 tablespoons apricot preserves
2 cups Vanilla Bean Whipped Cream (recipe follows)
2 to 3 tablespoons Candied Nuts (page 298)

recipe continues ⟶

VANILLA BEAN WHIPPED CREAM

1 cup heavy whipping cream
1 tablespoon sweetener (sugar, honey, or sorghum)
½ vanilla bean, scraped seeds only

Place the cream, sweetener, and vanilla seeds in a stainless-steel or glass bowl and whisk until billowy and thick. Whipping by hand will prevent overmixing. Mound onto the desired dessert.

TART DOUGH

MAKES ENOUGH FOR TEN TO TWELVE 4-INCH TARTLETS

3½ sticks unsalted butter, softened
¾ cup granulated sugar
1 egg
½ teaspoon pure vanilla extract
3¾ cups bread flour

Place the butter and sugar in the large bowl of an electric mixer. Beat with a paddle attachment until the mixture is light and fluffy. Add the egg and vanilla, then add the flour and mix on medium-low for about 30 seconds.

Remove the dough from the mixer and wrap in plastic. Allow to rest and cool in the fridge for at least 1 hour before using. The tart dough can be frozen for 1 to 2 months. The dough freezes best when it is rolled out and wrapped very tightly.

This dessert is a balance of sweet and spicy. It's an homage to a restaurant I learned a lot from back in the day, the now shuttered Café Henry Burger in Hull, Quebec. Chef Robert Bourassa was an amazing inspiration in how he ran the restaurant, being omnipresent and attentive in the business, and caring for its every move. This recipe, along with a braised halibut and a pheasant dish, still remains very clear in my mind from his repertoire.

I remember plating salads one night when the maître d' came rushing back to find out one of the patron's names. Thinking, probably rightly, that I was one of the few who would know about American political figures of the time, he tried to explain, in broken English, who the person was. "She is a lawyer. The top lawyer. She looks a little manly."

I knew immediately. Attorney General Janet Reno. She enjoyed her meal.

This is the perfect recipe for a warm summer evening with a nice Sauternes.

● ●

Warm a medium-size fry pan over medium heat. Once the pan is warm, add the butter and melt it just until it starts to froth and bubble.

Raise the heat to medium-high. Add the strawberries and sauté for about 2 minutes. Add the sugar and pepper and then deglaze with the Cointreau. You want the Cointreau to flame, but want to also keep your eyebrows intact. If you have an electric stove, you can use a match to create the flame. This will result in a nice syrup being created.

Remove from the heat and toss the mint into the strawberries.

Place a scoop of ice cream into 4 bowls. Evenly distribute the strawberries over the ice cream while the berries are still warm.

SERVES 4

SAUTÉED STRAWBERRIES
with black pepper & vanilla bean ice cream

2 tablespoons unsalted butter

2 pints strawberries, washed, hulled, and quartered

1 teaspoon granulated sugar

½ tablespoon cracked black peppercorn

1 shot Cointreau

Fresh mint, cut into chiffonnade, for garnish

1 pint Vanilla Bean Ice Cream (page 296)

I scream. You scream. We all scream for...

VANILLA BEAN ICE CREAM

1²/₃ cups whole milk
½ cup heavy whipping cream
½ cup granulated sugar
Pinch of salt
½ vanilla bean, scraped seeds and pod
3 egg yolks

"I scream, you scream, we all scream for ice cream!" There is a great scene in *Down by Law*, a wonderful Jim Jarmusch film that has Roberto Benigni, Tom Waits, and John Lurie chanting it together. I love ice cream, and while you can get some particularly great ice creams at the grocery store these days, there is still nothing like homemade ice cream after a great meal.

● ●

In a medium bowl, combine the milk, cream, ¼ cup of the sugar, the salt, and the vanilla seeds and pod. Pour this mixture into a medium saucepan over medium heat. Slowly warm the mixture, stirring occasionally until it begins to steam, 5 to 8 minutes, but do not let the mixture boil. Keep a very close eye on it.

Turn off the heat, cover, and let steep with the lid on for 30 minutes to infuse with flavor.

In a medium bowl, whisk together the remaining ¼ cup of sugar and the yolks until well blended and pale yellow. Slowly temper the warm liquid into the yolks and sugar a little at a time while whisking constantly. Slowly raising the temperature will prevent the eggs from scrambling. When at least half the liquid has been tempered into the yolks, pour the now warm yolk mixture in with the milk mixture in the saucepan.

Place the saucepan over low heat and stir constantly with a rubber spatula until the mixture is thick enough to coat the back of a spoon, 8 to 10 minutes.

Turn off the heat and strain the mixture immediately. Chill the mixture in the fridge and freeze according to your ice cream machine's directions.

MAKES 1 QUART

FLAVOR OPTIONS

Play around with all kinds of different flavors by steeping them in the milk and cream mixture. Try teas, herbs, spices, different nuts, coffee, and even cake scraps.

tip: toasting the nuts and spices before infusing into the milk will help extract flavor. Exclude the vanilla bean for all options.

CINNAMON: Toast a cinnamon stick in the oven to bring out the flavor. Add the stick to the milk and cream mixture and allow to steep. Follow the recipe as stated above and add 1 teaspoon ground cinnamon when you spin the ice cream.

PEANUT: Toast ½ cup peanuts and roughly chop them. Add them to the milk and cream mixture. Follow the recipe as stated above, and strain out the peanuts at the end and discard. Add the toasted peanuts after spinning if you prefer chunky over smooth.

SORGHUM: Substitute the first ¼ cup of sugar with sorghum. Bring it to a steam with the other ingredients. Follow the recipe as stated above. To serve, drizzle the ice cream with sorghum: Yum!

CANDIED NUTS

This is a Shae delight. Shae Rehmel is the wonderful pastry chef of Five and Ten and a very gifted baker. Her understanding of my food and how to match it with great desserts has been a beautiful relationship that has just always worked.

This is wonderful broken up onto ice cream or on its own as a great travel snack.

¼ cup plus 1 tablespoon granulated sugar
2 cups nuts of your choice: pistachios (best if blanched and peeled), almonds, hazelnuts (skinned), pecans, walnuts (better with small pieces), peanuts, or macadamia nuts

1 tablespoon honey
1 tablespoon light corn syrup
1 teaspoon ground cinnamon
1 teaspoon salt

Preheat the oven to 350°F.

Combine 1 tablespoon water and the 1 tablespoon of sugar in a medium saucepan over medium heat and stir to dissolve the sugar. Cook for 1 minute and remove from the heat. Off heat add to the saucepan the nuts, honey, corn syrup, cinnamon, salt, and the remaining ¼ cup of sugar and stir to combine.

Pour the mixture onto a rimmed baking sheet lined with a nonstick, flexible baking mat, such as a Silpat. Bake until the nuts are a nice deep golden brown, about 10 minutes. Check and rotate after 7 minutes.

Allow to cool, break apart, and then keep in an airtight container.

This is the cookie that we always made when I was young. Shae Rehmel, the saint of the pastry program at Five and Ten, has refined it into a wonderfully rich cookie that works every time. Simple and straightforward, it is a classic cookie that is my afternoon treat with an espresso.

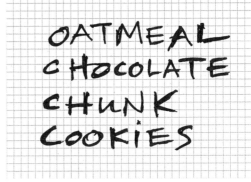

Preheat the oven to 350°F.

Place the butter in a small saucepan over low heat. Cook until melted.

Add the sugar, salt, vanilla, cinnamon, and melted butter to a large bowl and whisk for 2 minutes. Add the egg and egg yolk and whisk for 1 more minute. Let the mixture rest for 10 minutes.

In a small bowl, combine the oats, flour, and baking soda.

Give the butter and sugar mixture another whisk for 1 minute and then gently fold the flour mixture in. Once it is nicely incorporated, add the chocolate.

Divide the mixture into 10 portions and space 1½ inches apart on a parchment-lined baking sheet.

Bake for 6 minutes, rotate the pan, and bake for another 4 to 6 minutes. The cookies should be golden brown and still a little soft in the middle. Remove from the oven and transfer the cookies to a wire rack to cool completely. If you are not serving the cookies immediately, store them in an airtight container.

MAKES 10 LARGE COOKIES

½ cup (1 stick) unsalted butter

½ cup plus 1 tablespoon granulated sugar

½ teaspoon salt

1 teaspoon pure vanilla extract

½ teaspoon ground cinnamon

1 egg plus 1 egg yolk

1 cup rolled oats

¾ cup all-purpose flour

¼ teaspoon baking soda

1 (4-ounce) bar semisweet chocolate, cut or broken into small chunks

ACKNOWLEDGMENTS

This book would not have been possible without the help of so many fine people.

I am married to a wonderful woman named Mary, and we have two beautiful daughters, Beatrice and Clementine. They brighten every day with unquestioned support and love. Being married to a chef is never easy and Mary does it with unending grace.

To Lauren Johnson, assistant extraordinaire, who guides my days. Lauren is our marketing pro, our PR rep, our logic checker, and a great recipe tester.

To Rinne Allen, the gifted photographer of this book and the design guru who started all of this process by putting together a book proposal like no one had ever seen.

To Dean Neff, wonderful sous chef, who is always willing to work on any project and has always been my travel buddy. Dean's contribution to this book was immeasurable.

To Shae Rehmel, pastry chef of our dreams, who makes life sweeter for all of us at Five and Ten.

To Chuck Ramsey and Peter Dale, my amazingly talented team of executive chefs at Five and Ten, The National, and Empire State South.

To Ashley Malec, nanny, recipe tester, and longtime cook and bartender at Five and Ten, for being the sweetest and most patient culinary assistant, particularly when nine months pregnant.

To the waiters, hosts, and bussers who run the floors, particularly the A-Team.

To the cooks and chefs who learn every day.

To the fine folks at Clarkson Potter, particularly my editor, Emily Takoudes.

To Bertis Downs and Peter Smith, for great advice on a wide array of topics. I couldn't ask for a better team of friends who happen to be lawyers.

To the chefs who have taught me either through books or through their work: Frank Stitt, Ben Barker, Mario Batali, Mike Fennelly, and Rob MacDonald.

There are some people who just need shout-outs because they are awesome: Mimi Maumus, Lucy Gillis, Susan Hable, Jordan Noel, Steven Grubbs, Celia Barss, and my sisters, Kathy, Susie, and Rachel. Also Barbara and Sid for being great, supportive in-laws and keeping apprised of all South Carolina Lowcountry happenings.

To our wonderful blog recipe testers who gave great feedback through the recipes and were everything we asked for in a volunteer audience.

I am lucky to have a wonderful family in this world and particularly would like to thank my dad, Keith, for always being the greatest cheerleader of everything I have done in my adult life. He was less enthused about how I spent my teen years, but then again most parents are. Thanks, Dad.

index

NOTE: PAGE REFERENCES IN *ITALICS* INDICATE PHOTOGRAPHS.

TROUT

BACON
MUSTARD
CAPERS
FRISEE
BUTTER BEANS
CAMPFIRE TOMATOES
THYME

SALMON

LEMON
CAPERS
POTATOES
RADISHES
CUCUMBER
MUSTARD
BEETS
FENNEL

CHICKEN:

chervil
tarragon
pinenuts
celery
mushroom. butter
thyme
lemon
olive oil
grapes
risotto
stuffing
chestnuts

PORK

braise:

FRUIT / apples
pear
CABBAGE
SORGHUM
HOMINY GRITS.
CIDER vinegar
CHILES.
SAGE · MILK
FIGS
peppered mango
cooked tomato.